Crimes Against Children

A Guide to Child Protection
for Parents and Professionals

Featuring
The Little Rascals
Day Care Sex Scandal

David E. McCall
Child Abuse Investigator

RTP
Research Triangle Publishing

Published by
Research Triangle Publishing, Inc.
PO Box 1223
Fuquay-Varina, NC 27526

ISBN 1-884570-27-5

Library of Congress Catalog Card Number: 95-68229

Cover Design by
Kathy Holbrook

Printed in the United States of America
10 9 8 7 6 5 4 3 2 1

Written Contributions and Excerpts from Works by

Gloria Steinem, Author, *Revolution From Within*
Dr. Roland Summit, Expert, Child Sexual Abuse Accommo-
    dation Syndrome
Dr. Ken Magid, Psychologist, High Risk Children
Marilyn Van Derbur Atler, 1958 Miss America
Kimberly Crnich, Attorney
Debra Whitcomb, Senior Scientist, Educational Development
    Center
Betty Wade-Coyle, Executive Director, Hampton Roads Pre-
    vent Child Abuse Chapter
Dr. Robert Perry, Pediatrician
T. J., Incest Survivor
And other anonymous individuals.

My sincere love, thanks and appreciation go to my family, to written contributors to this project and to John—who has taught me more about children than have hundreds of hours of child protective services training.
    Confidentiality is not compromised in this publication. The facts are either part of court or public records or have been drawn from a composite of child protective services and experiences.

TEN COMMANDMENTS
FOR CHILD PROTECTION

1.	Interview The Child With Proper Interpretation.
2.	Interview The Child's Caregivers.
3.	Interview Relevant Collaterals.
4.	Make Home Visits.
5.	Use The Polygraph or Voiceprint If Relevant.
6.	Make Prompt Case Decisions.
7.	Make Appropriate Referrals For Treatment.
8.	Educate The Public.
9.	Expedite The Paperwork.
10.	People Should Not Injure Children By Hitting, Biting, Demeaning, Sexually Assaulting, Improperly Supervising Them, Abandoning Them Or Attempting To Care For Them With A Serious Unattended Illness or Addiction.

Keep the 10th commandment and the other nine will not be needed!

THE ABC'S OF SAFE DAY CARE

A center should encourage frequent unannounced visits.

Be sure there is a lot of visibility and few or no locks on the doors.

Child-staff ratios should be low. Ideal is 4-1 for youngest and 10-1 for older children.

Discuss the qualifications and background of the child caregivers.

Explore other options if something does not feel right and one begins to realize the center is really not practicing what it preaches.

CONTENTS

KNOWLEDGE IS POWER

One of the largest child sexual abuse cases in North Carolina and U.S. history originated in Edenton, North Carolina. Seven adults were indicted on more than four hundred charges of sexual abuse that may have involved as many as ninety children. Lessons learned from the McMartin preschool trial in California, however, resulted in narrowing the charges and trying the defendants separately.

The first trial began July 22, 1991, and passed through all four seasons of the year.

Robert Fulton Kelly, Jr., age forty-three, co-owner of the Little Rascals Day Care Center in Edenton, North Carolina—a historic town where many of this country's founding fathers resided two hundred years ago—was in jail on more than one-million dollar bond since June of 1989. His trial lasted nine months, making this the longest and most expensive trial in North Carolina history.

The prosecution presented eighty-three witnesses, and the defense presented sixty defense witnesses. The media coverage in North Carolina was extensive and created a seesaw of public opinion throughout the trial. However, near the end of the trial, damaging testimony was presented when Kelly's ex-wife, now living in California, testified.

She testified that Robert Kelly maintained a secret post office box in a town near Edenton. In the box she found a brochure of children ages five to twelve years engaged in a number of sexual acts. She also stated Kelly was obsessed with pornography, watching it four or five nights a week. She testified Kelly called her up after their divorce and requested her to send him her dirty underwear.

In Farmville, North Carolina, after fourteen days of deliberation, exactly nine months after Robert Fulton Kelly, Jr. went on trial for sexually abusing children at the Little Rascals Day Care Center in Edenton, North Carolina, Kelly was convicted on ninety-nine of one hundred felony counts involving the sexual abuse of children—April 22, 1992. On April 23, he was sentenced to twelve consecutive life terms—the longest sentence handed down in North Carolina's judicial history. He would be eligible for parole in two hundred and forty years. As an initial social services investigator in the Robert Kelly case, I believe justice was served with this verdict.

What happened to the other six defendants? Or how about dozens of other unrelated cases in this historic little southern town known ironically as the "Cradle of the Colony?" The pages that follow represent the darkest moments in the lives of children. It must be read so that the lives and welfare of tomorrow's children might shine forth with love, hope and justice.

A child molester's "thrill" is found in his or her power over the victim—using knowledge as a tool. The same weapons are required in the war against child abuse. Use the information gained from this landmark case and scores of other crimes against children to increase your knowledge and power for the protection of children.

SCANDALS IN PARADISE

Beautiful Historic Edenton

EDENTON, CHOWAN COUNTY, NORTH CAROLINA
Founded 1672
Incorporated 1722

In its more than three centuries since European settlement, the historic little town of Edenton, North Carolina, has survived many aberrations. Voluminous documentation affirms a people trusting the courts to settle human differences. The same documentation attests to numerous cases of one person's powerful perpetration of sadistic will upon another.

The State Gazette, which located in Edenton in the late eighteenth century, kept citizens abreast of news occurring throughout the thirteen states and even from abroad. Some tidbits sounded like the tabloids one skims today while standing in the supermarket checkout line. For instance: "NORFOLK. October 5, 1797. Died. Lately in Iveraah, Ireland, aged 112, Daniel Bull MCCARTHY, Esq.. He was married to five wives; he married the fifth, who survives him, when he was 84, and she 14, by whom he had 20 children, bearing a child every year." Closer to home: "RICHMOND. December 19, 1797. Married on the 13th ultimo, by the Rev. Mr. CHASTAIN, Alexander MITCHELL, Esq. aged 109 years, much afflicted with the palsy, to the amiable and accomplished Miss Jane HAMMOND, aged 16 years, both of Buckingham county." One can only shudder at the fates of these two young women.

Interestingly, streakers have been around for awhile. *The North Carolinian Weekly*, published in Elizabeth City and circulated in Edenton, ran this piece in its January 8, 1873 issue.

"An excited young man, clad only in a pair of slippers, recently rushed into a church shouting 'Here I come in the name of Jesus.' He was taken out in the name of the law."

Now, in spite of the sorrow in their midst, Edenton residents continue to go through the motions required of responsible people earning a livelihood and attending to commitments. They do not relish the adverse attention brought about because of the Little Rascals Day Care case, such as the "Salem witch-hunt" label some disbelievers of the victims claim.

Neither do they fear the town will collapse because of name calling. A town that narrowly escaped destruction by British troops in the eighteenth century, Union troops in the nineteenth century, struggled through the Great Depression and sent its sons and daughters to fight in two world wars in the twentieth century knows firsthand what constitutes anguish.

Actually, Edenton has aged gracefully, developing roots able to withstand the inevitable as well as the unexpected. It has progressed from a lively seaport village, hosting a cosmopolitan lot of sailors, to a genteel Victorian hamlet whose inhabitants delighted in romanticizing their ancestors with veiled shrouds of aristocracy, to a town delighting thousands yearly with its slow-paced historic ambiance.

No doubt the court system, which has prevailed in the area since at least 1672, fifty years before "Ye Towne on Queen Anne's Creek" incorporated as Edenton, helped to establish these roots. Colonial records prove early settlers brought their British love of law to their wilderness home. Without it, North Carolina may have lagged years behind in becoming the civilized colony that in 1697 found Mary Rookes innocent of witchcraft. Furthermore, the court ordered damages awarded Rookes from her accuser for defaming her character.

In 1703, Thomas Bourchier did his best to convince a grand jury that Susannah Evans was a witch. Again, justice triumphed. The jury found Evans innocent, as did another jury in a like accusation against Martha Richardson.

A witch-hunt did not take place in Edenton in 1989, nor did a jury believe one had taken place when it found Robert Fulton Kelly, Jr. guilty on ninety-nine counts of child sexual abuse in 1992.

The state's motto, *Esse Quam Videri* (To Be Rather Than Seem), aptly fits the native North Carolinian's predilection for using "good common sense." Described as being a vale of humility located between the aristocratic states of Virginia and South Carolina, North Carolina produced an independent people quite capable of thinking for themselves.

In 1712, surveyor, attorney and planter Edward Moseley laid out the original design of the town in an English village plan, complete with a commons footing at the edge of Edenton Bay. Today, three twenty-four-pound cannons from the Revolutionary period present a well-fortified appearance to vessels entering the harbor. The Old Chowan County Courthouse, built in 1767 and described as the finest Georgian courthouse in the South, stands at the head of the commons, also known as the "publick parade" and currently as the courthouse green. Edenton prospered as the "metropolis" (the first capital) of North Carolina (1722-43).

During the prime years of Edenton's "Golden Age" (1740-1781), some remarkable men chose to make the town their home. At age seventeen, James Iredell Sr. arrived from Bristol, England, to be comptroller of the port. In 1790, Iredell, who read the law under his brother-in-law's tutelage, was appointed to serve as judge on the First United States Supreme Court.

Iredell's Scottish-born brother-in-law, Samuel Johnston, was, among many other offices, a governor of North Carolina (1787-89) and a U.S. senator (1790-93). His home, Hayes, designed by British architect William Nichols, is a National

Historic Landmark. Johnston served reluctantly as president of the United States for a day, eight years prior to the election of George Washington.

Princeton educated Joseph Hewes came to town in the 1750s from his New Jersey home near Princeton. A merchant, postmaster, shipbuilder and statesman, Hewes' peers described him as "a man with good common sense." As a delegate to the First Continental Congress, Hewes was a signer of the Declaration of Independence. He was also secretary of the Naval Affairs Committee of the Continental Congress, virtually the first secretary of the navy and patron/mentor to John Paul Jones.

Another outstanding person who lived for a time in Edenton was Dr. Hugh Williamson of Pennsylvania. The talented Williamson preached; wrote books; taught mathematics; practiced medicine (he served as surgeon general of the North Carolina troops in 1779); conducted scientific experiments, including the kite and key electrical experiment with Dr. Benjamin Franklin; and actively participated in politics. A delegate to the Continental Congress (1782-85), the Federal Convention (1787-89) and an elected member of the First U.S. Congress, Dr. Williamson was one of the three signers of the U.S. Constitution for North Carolina.

While the men were busy fighting—literally, politically or both—for the nation's freedom, a group of local women held the earliest known instance of purely political activity on the part of women in the American colonies. On October 25, 1774, fifty-one women from Edenton and the surrounding Albemarle area counties affixed their signatures to a document stating their support of action taken by the First North Carolina Provincial Congress to boycott English tea, cloth and other commodities. Unlike the better known "Boston Tea Party," the "Edenton Tea Party" took place in a civil and orderly fashion with the identity of its participants signed in ink.

Visitors often comment, "It must be wonderful to live in Paradise." To these people, perhaps it seems like paradise as they stroll along quiet streets lined by ancient oaks shadowing the elegance of past ages, as they pass well-kept lawns fronting eighteenth and nineteenth-century homes, inhale the sweet breath of wisteria and magnolia and watch playful squirrels leap from tree to tree landing among ruffled branches of flowering crape myrtles.

One is grateful for the beauty of Edenton, but life afflicts people here just as it does anyone, anywhere. A more realistic portrayal of Edenton's past indicates that some of its citizens were not always kind. According to public record, in July 1737, Elizabeth Abel, proprietress of a "Lew'd and disorderly Tippleling house Contrary to law," was "tyed to a carts tayl and whipt out of the Town by receiving thirty lashes on her bare back well laid on." Abel was ordered never to return to Edenton. Shortly thereafter, in 1742, Mary Berry was whipped out of town "at the cart's arse" on an accusation of stealing.

Husbands accusing their wives of nagging could have the poor souls "ducket" in the stagnated, "publick ducking pool," which also accommodated the town tannery. In 1980, the new Chowan County Courthouse and jail were constructed on this property.

Across the street from these buildings stands the James Iredell House State Historic Site (circa 1774). Although a charming place to visit today, to enjoy during Christmas with its period decorations and lavish "groaning board" open house, Judge Iredell's home did not always reverberate with sounds of merriment.

Iredell's letters attest to many adverse circumstances in his and his family's lives. In a letter to his uncle, Thomas Iredell of Jamaica, the judge describes his youngest daughter, Helen. Having said how industrious and intelligent Helen's older brother and sister are, Iredell writes: "My youngest child is a daughter nearly four, and I have reason to flatter myself will be equal to the other two. I thank God all their dispositions appear to be good." Yet, a few years later, Helen became so uncontrollable, she was sent to New England to live with a physician who cared for the mentally deranged.

From top to bottom, the windows in Helen's upstairs bedroom at the Iredell House retain holes indicating, perhaps, they were boarded up on the inside to protect the child from jumping out and harming herself.

A caring man, some of Iredell's accounts mention the misfortunes of others he encountered while traveling the circuit as a judge. His narratives transcend time, depicting the sufferings and the pleasures of human existence.

Two of the great pleasures of Iredell's time and into the next century were weddings and funerals. Both afforded opportunity for socializing. When a death occurred, the courthouse bell would toll, alerting the community to prepare for the funeral master's arrival. Ladies anxiously awaited the black man's knock on the door to receive an invitation.

One century later on November 6, 1894, in St. Paul's Episcopal Church, Cora Estelle Mitchell, twenty-four, of Edenton wed Dr. Joseph Adrian Booth, fifty-four, of New York City in one of the more prominent weddings in Edenton history. An account in the *Fisherman & Farmer*, a local newspaper, described it as "one of the most brilliant social events that has taken place in Edenton for years, and attended by Dr. Booth's many friends from all over the country." The dark side to this connection was the groom's relation to the assassin of one of this nation's most loved Presidents.

Dr. Booth was the son of Junius Brutus Booth, the great Shakespearean actor, and the younger brother of John Wilkes Booth, assassin of President Lincoln, and of Edwin Booth, the renowned actor. He was also his bride's cousin through her father's, Col. R. G. Mitchell's, side of the family.

One of Edenton's sex scandals of the nineteenth century received its fullest revelation in 1987 with the publishing by the Harvard University Press of *Incidents In The Life of a Slave Girl: Written by Herself* by Harriet A. Jacobs. First published in 1861 by a Boston publisher, Jacobs book was edited by L. Maria Child. The recent edition was edited by Jean Fagin Yellin, who added illustrations, an extensively researched chronology, letters written by and to Harriet Jacobs and documented notes identifying people and places Jacobs thinly disguised in her text with fictitious names. Considered abolitionist propaganda by some people in both centuries, Yellin's research appears to substantiate a great deal of Jacob's account.

Born in 1813 to Delilah, a slave of Margaret Horniblow of Edenton, and Daniel Jacobs, a slave of Dr. Andrew Knox of nearby Perquimans County, Harriet Jacobs was taught to read, spell and sew by her mistress, Mrs. Horniblow. When the latter died in 1825, she willed Jacobs to her three-year-old niece, Mary Matilda Norcom, daughter of Edenton physician James Norcom.

According to Jacobs, by 1829 Dr. Norcom (Dr. Flint in her narrative) appeared intent on making her his concubine. She was sixteen years old. She fought off his advances, realizing many of his conquests were sold with their newborns so that he might not have to explain to a jealous wife about the resemblance between himself and young slave children living at Auburn, his plantation.

Samuel Tredwell Sawyer (Mr. Sands in her narrative), a future United States congressman living in Edenton, fathered two of her children. Hidden in the attic of her grandmother's home for a period of seven years, Jacobs finally escaped to the northern states. Norcom seemed intent on doing everything he could to recapture the young slave girl.

Jacob's book promotes much of the abolitionist thought during the Civil War period. It is also invaluable for understanding the dehumanizing and demeaning nature of the institution of slavery and the role that sexual improprieties played in the perpetuation of that despicable institution.

Knowing how many instances have occurred in Edenton (or for that matter anyplace where humans dwell) of one person's power play at another's expense—whether sexual, sadistic, covetous or egotistical—remains an improbability known only to the Almighty. "The Cradle of the Colony," for all its attributes, is not a paradise, but a typical American town that exemplifies the good and the bad that permeates the American fabric.

Surrounding the historical importance of the Robert Fulton Kelly, Jr. trial is the fact that a Salem-style witch-hunt did not occur and a perpetrator of crimes against children was justly convicted. A significant battle in the war against crimes of child sexual abuse was fought and won in Edenton.

Many casualties occurred. Healing will only begin with an acceptance of history being not merely a person, a place or a remembered event of great import. Rather, it is a process having a mixture of good and bad, teaching us how to strive for that ultimate goal where the truth is always known and children are always safe.

SIGNS OF THE TIMES

Depending on the statistician, one might discover child sexual abuse ratios as high as one in three or as low as one in ten children who are sexually abused by age eighteen.

Here is my statistic—Child sexual abuse is epidemic! During my first four years as a child protective services investigator (CPS), I became aware of one new victim of sexual abuse per month on average. That does not include the ninety children who were involved in the Little Rascals day care case. This figure for the child population is sixty-eight times the rate of reported cases of AIDS for the entire Chowan County population.

There are critics, especially in the editorial media, who have stated the epidemic is in the number of false accusations of child sexual abuse. They claim investigations regularly ruin the lives and careers of innocent people. They neither understand the issues surrounding the sexual abuse of children, nor do they make any appropriate attempts to understand those issues.

My experience with false accusations is minimal because the occurrence of false accusations is minimal. There were only two cases where false accusations could be implied but would not be accurate during that four year period.

In one case, a child changed the disclosure. In another case, the perpetrator could not be accurately identified. This does not mean the crime did not take place. It means that identifying the criminal was a major problem with this case as it is with many crimes. These investigations, conducted in the same professional manner as the Little Rascals case, did not wreck anyone's career.

My most serious encounters with false accusations in recent years involved several unrelated cases involving nine-year-old children who told outright lies that were easily verifiable as untrue. However, even in these cases, understanding the basis behind the false stories was uncovered in the investigative process. It usually involved some type of anxiety caused by an incident unrelated to the allegation—but also unrelated to any type of abuse. I call it "displaced anxiety." It has helped me understand this particular phenomena in CPS investigations.

Also, I have investigated sexual abuse cases involving children under the age of six years where a child's disclosure was not properly interpreted or understood by well-meaning adults. There is usually some basis for the child's statement, and the investigator must be able to determine the reason for the disclosure. Determining the basis will clear an innocent person or place a guilty person in jail. My job has involved both scenarios.

Sometimes one discovers the child literally means what the child states. One may find the child repeating information the child has heard. If not properly interviewed, the child may add details that in the child's mind may seem reasonable but are not factual. Be careful, however. These are also common excuses used by guilty perpetrators. Sometimes the basis for the disclosure may never be discovered.

When interviewing the alleged perpetrator, one should try to determine if the reaction to the allegation is natural or part of an act. If he or she is a candidate for the "Oscars," you may be able to determine a motive for the performance. Many perpetrators have natural reactions which provide near or complete admissions, making the investigator's job much easier.

My suggestion is to use a polygraph or voiceprint analysis so some confidence in direction can be obtained. One may scrutinize the usefulness of a polygraph, but it does improve the odds for a successful investigation.

The Little Rascals case is a sign of the times. The number of lives that have been directly affected by the alleged obsession of Robert Fulton Kelly, Jr. is a testimony to the epidemic nature of child sexual abuse in America. His initial conviction is a sign that there is justice in this country.

What are the signs of the times? What are the signs of child sexual abuse? This is perhaps the most often asked question during seminars on child sexual abuse. People want to know the trade secrets of child sexual abuse investigators concerning the identification of both victims and perpetrators. They know there must be some kind of code that can be broken by the top experts in the field. Teachers, parents and even "new" social workers want to know those telltale signs that are privileged information among professional investigators.

Here is a list of signs. I list them reluctantly, not because this is privileged information, but because one disclosure is worth more than one hundred indicators when conducting an investigation.

CHILD SEXUAL ABUSE INDICATORS—Obvious indicators like venereal disease, pregnancy or physical injury are often not present. There are many forms of sexual abuse that do not require forceful assault. Also, all children face behavioral changes. It was the severity and the duration of the behavioral changes that were significant in the Little Rascals case—forty-five minute screaming sessions, night terrors and sexually explicit acting out.

1. Venereal Disease
2. Genital or Anal Injury
3. Pregnancy and Sperm Presence

4. Severe Mood Swings
5. Significant Behavioral Changes
6. Sexual Knowledge Inconsistent with Age
7. Low Self-esteem
8. Fears—Expressed Many Ways
9. Promiscuity
10. Sleep Disorders (Nightmares, Bedwetting, etc.)
11. Excessive Masturbation

The purpose in knowing the signs is to help us understand that a child may be at risk. One does not need to be a professional to learn this. Being observant of one's children and involved with one's children is the primary skill. Developing a strong trusting relationship between parent and child is important. The sex abuser develops this relationship in order to take advantage of the child. The investigator tries to establish this relationship to gain information. The prosecutors and defense attorneys make similar attempts to establish rapport.

One must take the signs at face value. They are just signs—signs that something is wrong. Stress can be caused by many factors, and most of these signs are indicators of stress.

Also, in many cases involving children with attention deficit hyperactivity disorder (ADHD) and Tourette Syndrome (TS), I have discovered sexual acting-out behaviors that are many times unrelated to any kind of abuse. I have also found that these children's disclosures must be closely examined. However, this does not mean one should rule out a thorough and complete investigation if an allegation involves one of these children. They often are victims of abuse and neglect, especially when proper intervention dealing with their special needs has not taken place.

It is difficult to determine who the perpetrator is or pinpoint the specific reason why the signs are there unless there is a disclosure by the child. Other than the perpetrator, the child is usually the only other witness to the crime committed. The disclosures in the Little Rascals case were extremely important to the investigation. Before rumors spread and without the use of leading or loaded questions, many children made statements that substantially corroborated each other's disclosures. Corroborating disclosure is ideal.

Knowing the signs of sexual abuse is important, but it is also important to learn how state laws define sexual crimes. The following important statutes relate directly to sexual crimes that involve children in the state of North Carolina and correspond with similar statutes in other states.

Selected Statutes Pertaining to Child Sex Crimes in North Carolina: The following includes excerpts as it would be impossible to include all the information provided in the North Carolina statutes. The laws are effective as of October 1, 1993. Statute 7A-517. Abused Juveniles. Any juvenile less than eighteen years of age whose parent, guardian, custodian or caretaker:

- Inflicts or allows to be inflicted upon the juvenile a physical injury by other than accidental means.

- Creates or allows to be created a substantial risk of physical injury to the juvenile by other than accidental means.

- Uses or allows to be used upon the juvenile cruel or grossly inappropriate procedures or cruel or grossly inappropriate devices to modify behavior.

- Commits, permits or encourages the commission of a violation of the following laws by, with or upon the juvenile; (statute numbers are deleted) first-degree rape, second-degree rape, first-degree sexual offense, second-degree sexual offense, sexual act by a custodian, crime against nature, incest, preparation of obscene photographs, slides or motion pictures of the juvenile, employing or permitting the juvenile to assist in a violation of the obscenity laws, dissemination of obscene material to the juvenile, displaying or disseminating material harmful to the juvenile, first-and second-degree sexual exploitation of the juvenile, promoting the prostitution of the juvenile, and taking indecent liberties with the juvenile, regardless of age of the parties.

- Creates or allows to be created serious emotional damage to the juvenile. Serious emotional damage is evidenced by a juvenile's severe anxiety, depression, withdrawal or aggressive behavior toward himself or others.

- Encourages, directs or approves of delinquent acts involving moral turpitude committed by the juvenile.

Elements of Proof—To convict a defendant of a first-degree sexual offense with a child of twelve years or less, the state need only prove that (1) the defendant engaged in a "sexual act," (2) the victim was at the time of the act twelve years old or less, and (3) the defendant was at that time four or more years older than the victim. State v. Ludlum.

Testimony of Four Year Old Victim Sufficient Evidence of Cunnilingus—Testimony of four-year-old girl that defendant "touched me...with his tongue...between my legs," while indicating the place of touching to the jury, constituted sufficient evidence of cunnilingus to support a conviction for a first-degree sexual offense. State v. Ludlum. "Sexual act" means cunnilingus, fellatio, analingus or anal intercourse, but does not include vaginal intercourse. Sexual act also means the penetration, however slight, by any object into the genital or anal opening of another person's body: provided, that it shall be an affirmative defense that the penetration was for accepted medical purposes.

Sexual crimes are punishable as felonies and some carry mandatory life sentences.

Many sex offenders do not realize they have committed felonies, but careful reading of the North Carolina statutes and their definitions will clarify any misconceptions concerning their activities. The explanation that "sexual act" includes penetration by any object, no matter how slight, was a key focus of the Little Rascals case.

Children testified about varying degrees of penetration. Many of the charges related to inappropriate touching that did not leave evidence were still considered to be against the law.

Several children did show physical evidence of sexual abuse consistent with their disclosures, according to child medical examiners. The evidence allegedly ranged, according to medical examiners, from mild to severe indications of penetration—anal and vaginal scarring, anal dilation and asymmetrical attenuation of the hymen.

Mr. Kelly continued to maintain his innocence. Mr. Kelly allegedly told the media he wanted the children to know he did not harm them, and he testified in court that he never touched the children in a sexual way. However, according to twelve corroborative witnesses, the North Carolina statutes and twelve jurors, Mr. Kelly was found guilty of sexual offenses against children.

A key word to understand is "intent." What is the intent of the action of an adult towards a child. Bathing a child would not constitute a charge of sexual abuse, but fondling a child for purposes of either sexual gratification or sadistic satisfaction is an infringement.

The children in the Little Rascals case could only discuss the action of the adult(s) involved, not their intent. Without a law degree readily available, one can only rely on common sense to determine the actions were not the result of simple hugging, bathing or changing diapers. Twelve jurors came to that same rational conclusion.

Most addicts do not feel they have a problem. Likewise in denial are sex offenders of children and many times their spouses or supporters, but let's save this for the lesson on perpetrators. The point is the law is clearly defined, and perpetrators should beware of the signs of the times.

It is extremely difficult to obtain a conviction in a multi-perpetrator, multi-victim case like the Little Rascals case or the McMartin preschool trial in California. The McMartin preschool trial, with all of its publicity and ultimate failure to obtain a conviction, forced prosecutors across the country to stay away from prosecuting such complex cases.

Child advocates wonder if the conviction of Robert Fulton Kelly, Jr. will change the attitude of prosecutors by showing them proper methods can be utilized to obtain an appropriate conviction, even if felons win appeals.

CONCLUSION: Child sexual abuse is epidemic. It has been the best kept secret among sex offenders and their victims for thousands of years. There is no witch-hunt hysteria in this country concerning sexual abuse, except among critics too misdirected to realize a serious problem exists. They remain on a perpetual witch-hunt or as some call it, "a lamb hunt." They slaughter children and their families who have already been victimized by someone they trusted by saying they are fantasizing the abuse or brainwashed into believing they were abused. False accusations do occur but competent investigations will ultimately obtain the truth.

Signs are important indicators that something is wrong, but identification of the perpetrator with the child's disclosure is the key element in an investigation. There was a case where a child had a pleasing personality and made straight "A's" in school while living in a horrible environment. Several years passed before the child disclosed sexual abuse and the perpetrator confessed. Good grades in school could actually be considered a "sign" in this case because school served as a coping mechanism for abuse and neglect at home. However, little effective action occurred until the disclosure was made. Signs come in various forms and are very difficult to read.

The initial conviction of Robert Fulton Kelly, Jr. should be a sign of the changes in the perception of child sexual abuse and in the ability of competent prosecutors to handle cases this size. The law is no longer just on the books; it is now upheld in the judicial system. The law is clear. You cannot commit sexual acts with children or you will go to jail.

IT COULD HAPPEN TO ANYONE

THE VICTIM—The actions of a crime touch everyone. Sexual crimes involving children are no different. In fact, the effect of a sexual crime against a child can be felt for generations. It is true that many perpetrators were victims as children. However, this does not mean children who are victimized will become perpetrators.

Like "dominoes" the chain can be broken—through professional help or through other coping mechanisms the child naturally develops. Some victims develop coping mechanisms that can be self-destructive, while others may develop mechanisms that are very positive. Still others may fall into that group that acts out the same abuse imposed upon themselves. This last group unfortunately is the basis for the domino theory of child abuse in America. It affects people in every direction and passes from one generation to the next.

The greatest chance to successfully break the chain of abuse depends on that word discussed earlier—"trust." Those who wonder why sex with children is wrong need to read carefully. Yes, there are organized groups that promote sex with children. Serving their own interests, they fail to realize the severe breach of trust that occurs.

Whether it is sexual abuse, neglect, physical abuse or emotional abuse, the net effect on a child is destruction of trust. Sometimes the destruction takes immediate effect, sometimes it is delayed until the child reaches certain developmental realizations. It attacks and eats away the trust components in the conscious and subconscious mind.

Several years ago, a young man in his early twenties complained how his grandfather had touched him and other children in the family while they were growing up. The family was shocked that dear "ole grandpa" could be accused of child abuse and responded, "He has always played with the kids like that—just playing around you know." This is a perfect example of how someone can abuse children without considering it to be abusive. The case was easily substantiated, because everyone admitted to the alleged actions. The "touching" was totally inappropriate. Let it suffice to say grandpa wasn't just "patting the children on the head."

Just as trust can be destroyed by abusive situations, it can be rebuilt with positive, loving trust-restoring processes. Some victims will attain this through natural circumstances, but many will need to receive professional help. That is why therapists are adamantly recommended as soon as possible when abuse is discovered. The sooner trust is reestablished, the sooner recovery can begin.

Examine the following excerpts from *The Holding Therapy Handbook* by Dr. Ken Magid and begin to understand the trust issues and the problems that can occur with severely abused and neglected children. Note, a child with a severe attachment disorder may not have an obvious case background of severe abuse or neglect, but something significant in the child's past has occurred. Also, biological factors may play a role.

"THE TOP 33—An Updated List of Symptoms For Children With Severe Attachment Disorder."

- Infants generally manifest a stiffness and inability to connect with others. Children learn not to trust adults. Look for a history of significant breaks in the attachment cycle.

- Cruelty to others (often without apparent motive). Often threatens harm to others.

- Cruelty to pets (although sometimes bonds to a selected animal).

- Destruction to property (both to others and their own).

- Self-mutilation and high pain tolerance (although seldom carries out suicidal threats).

- Accident prone and careless.

- Inability to internalize the concept of love (although mimics role models if advantageous).

- Chronic stealing and occasional hoarding (often taking things that are not needed).

- Addictions to food, especially sugars (gorging but not purging).

- Sensory integration problems.

- Attraction to negative power bases and the dark side (including satanism, violent media, victim pain, death and anything feared by others).

- Child can demonstrate acceptable behavior for short periods of time and seem "normal."

- Absence of enduring or genuine long-term friendships. Attracted to other children with attachment disorders.

- Proclivity to thrill seeking and danger. Impulsive.

- Chronic lying and misrepresentations (often without apparent motive).

- Verbally adept at manipulation. Verbal scales overcompensated.

- Selective speech regression. Regressive baby talk or mumbling.

- Speech pathology (if early organic trauma).
- Hypnotic attractiveness to strangers (able to con the unsuspecting). Can be extremely charming and convincing.
- Eye aversion problems (reduced as child gets older).
- Cause-effect learning problems (doesn't readily learn from consequences).
- Must be in control of others (cannot be vulnerable).
- Inflated self-concept and grandiose thinking (illusions of grandeur).
- Negative drawings, usually pertaining to the release of rage on others, along with pictures of the devil, guns, bloody knives and bizarre consequences.
- Self-deceptive (belief in own fabrications).
- Sabotages organized plans and looks for power struggles with authority figures or other leaders. Frequently "out of control."
- Lack of remorse or genuine empathy.
- Preoccupation with sex and perversion (especially if history of molestation).
- Fascination with their own feces and inappropriate toilet behavior. They are often encopretic and enuretic.
- Fascination with fire (often with early history of arson).
- Resists physical closeness unless it's on their own terms.
- Can be provoked to uncontrollable rage.
- Combines several DSM disorders (often including conduct disorder, reactive attachment disorder and attention deficit-hyperactivity disorder).

"It's important to note that the appearance of one or two symptoms does not automatically categorize a child as having an attachment disorder. The onset of the symptoms, the number and type of symptoms, the duration, the severity and many other factors determine the diagnosis. An attachment disorder can be classified as mild, moderate and severe. If observed at certain times, these children can appear helpful, loving and emotionally stable. At other times the same children may seem almost non-human. Generally, one has to live with an unattached child to experience the full measure of this frequent transition. Treatment modalities may differ but all must help the child learn how to love and trust again. Please note that there is a separate profile for infants and adults." (For more information and research updates please contact the High Risk Child Foundation, 13131 West Cedar, Lakewood, Colorado 80228.)

Part of Robert Kelly's defense was the idea that therapists were used to place ideas in children's minds. This was not the case. Six of the twelve children who testified were part of the earliest stages of the investigation long before they went to therapists, and their information in court two and a half years later was consistent with many of their earliest disclosures. The children went to therapists as early as possible for their own welfare. Further disclosures came, and a competent prosecutor could not and would not ignore the reports being made. Therapists had to deal with the trust Robert Kelly destroyed.

Neither was there a conspiracy to manipulate the children's disclosures. Therapists and investigators attempted to place all the children's statements in the record. The numerous references to unbelievable activities like "killing babies" and "snakes" demonstrate the objectivity of the human service workers.

Children also later said the baby was a doll or the snake a prop. These statements were made along with those outlined in the "Bill of Particulars" later in this chapter. There is only one explanation for them—Robert Fulton Kelly, Jr. and others were allegedly sexually exploiting children for the purpose of pornography and sadistic and/or sexual satisfaction.

Unfortunately, Kelly had a lot of support and trust from the community, and had several months available to potentially "clean house" before a search warrant was issued. In fact, his teenage child was allegedly placed on an airplane to California two days after he was officially advised of the investigation.

The domino effect in the Little Rascals case or any abuse/neglect case is obvious in a small town like Edenton. A good example is a recent trip to a local supermarket where there were two mothers who had severely neglected their children, three convicted child molesters, and two victims of abuse—all unrelated and not connected to the Little Rascals case. However I later began to notice twelve other people who were, in some way connected to the Little Rascals case (people who were relatives of victims or relatives of people charged in the case). Ninety children and their relatives and friends—seven defendants and their relatives and friends—thousands of lives in a county of only 12,000 people have been greatly affected.

Almost everyone in some way feels victimized. Parents and relatives are victims, because the trust they placed in the Little Rascals Day Care Center and its owners, Robert and Betsy Kelly, was utterly destroyed. Children were told by their parents to listen to the child caregivers and to do as they were told—not realizing their parents would disapprove of Kelly's actions.

In the mind of a small child, the omnipotent parent knows all and sees all and consequently should have known what "Mr.

Bob" was doing. The guilt parents felt for "not knowing" was another issue the families had to suffer through.

Some parents suffered an additional breach of trust. They continued to support the Kellys for three months after the initial investigation and substantiation of abuse. They sent flowers, paid extra to keep the center operating and cooked meals for the Kellys. These same parents later alleged that they had been told lies about each other by the Kellys and heard their own children tell sordid details about abuse at the day care center.

One parent served as Bob Kelly's attorney until discovering his own child's involvement. Another parent heard his/her child disclose information about abuse, but continued to support the center until the child disclosed further information and graphic demonstrations.

Some negative editorial coverage further victimized these parents. Claims that parents were on a "runaway train" chasing down the Kellys in a modern day "witch-hunt" is not credible especially in the face of the trust parents continued to place with the center for so long.

The following material demonstrates the "trust betrayed." Letters were sent to parents by Betsy Kelly in February and April of 1989 thanking them for their support. Letters were sent and comments were made by parents and grandparents in support of the center during this three-month period. The following is a paraphrase of typical comments made during this tragic case.

I wish to give my point of view about Little Rascals. It is the best day care in Edenton. My child has learned a lot since the center has been operating.

The workers have shown a lot of care and concern for the children and have always operated with the utmost integrity.

Please consider my comments as support in any determinations you may make about Little Rascals.

The following is excerpted from a letter written on July 9, 1989 from one parent to another. Names are substituted with parenthetical descriptions. Permission was given to reprint this letter.

Dear (parent's name),
I would like to start by saying that (your child) has been in my prayers for a long time, and I hope that (your child) is doing well in therapy now. I have prayed for all the children, that they can be healed from the horror of this situation. I thought that we were friends and our children were friends. I feel that I owe it to myself and to you to explain why you have been a great disappointment to me. (My child) is the most precious and dear thing to me, just as (your child) is to you. The abuse (my child) suffered did not come totally from the day care, however, for you consciously and maliciously (as an adult) helped damage an innocent child's reputation. Think for a moment how you would feel if this had been done to your child instead of mine.
Ever since our (children) have gone to Little Rascals, Betsy Kelly constantly talked to me about other children [and I must tell you that (yours) was tops on the list]. Last Fall I even called Betsy to tell her that I did not want to hear about other children, but I did need to know about any problems mine was having. I knew (my child) was being talked about, too. It didn't take too many brains to figure out that if others were being talked about so badly, (my child) wasn't being left out. I also was picking up bad vibes from a lot of people. When I confronted Betsy with this, she put the whole thing on you. She told me that you called her every night to find out what (my child) had done to (your child) that day. She said you were driving her crazy and

that she had finally told all her staff not to tell you anything. (A worker) was telling me things like—(your child) is ten times worse than (my child), but you can't tell his mother that; or (that you) said you don't want (my child) playing with (your child); and (your child) is picking up bad habits from (my child); and (your child) is influenced more by (my child) than the other way around.

(You) don't think that (my child) did not come home at night and tell me things (your child) did to (him/her)—(he/she) did. I thought it was kids being kids and probably being together too much. I certainly never took those things to others to hurt (your child) as you did mine. Of course, (my child) was having problems [and still is], and now I know why.

It was horrible enough that my (child) had been so terribly abused, but to also be so betrayed by people I thought were friends was too much to bear. (My child) could not understand for so many months why (her/his) friends still went to Little Rascals. (My child) still does not understand why some friends are not friends any longer. It was not our decision that things changed. Things could have been so different.

I have been hoping for the last two or three months that you would have the compassion and humility to come to me to apologize and try to undo some of the hurts you have caused. I see now even more that you are not the person I used to think you were. You have to live with your hypocrisy, though, not me. You can go through life making excuses for your denial if you want, but please leave my (child) out of it. (My child) has been hurt way too much already.

If this letter sounds harsh, it is because I have a lot of anger and hurt to work through. With the Lord's help I will find it in my heart to forgive you one day, but I will never forget.

(Note: The parents resolved their issues and began to heal when their children's testimony placed the blame where it belongs—with the conviction of Robert Fulton Kelly, Jr.)

The following letter was dictated by a child victim on July 19, 1991, three days before trial.

Dear Judge,
I'm glad that Mr. Bob's in jail because he did bad things. I want you to keep him in jail for the rest of his life. Mr. Bob made me feel sad. Mr. Bob made me angry. I would like to beat him up bad, bad, bad—until he is an old man. Don't let him ask what he wants to eat. Feed him liver everyday, and also dog food soup, or macaroni soup, and cat food salad, and bird seed and sand.
And he should stay in jail for the rest of his life and be with bad, bad guys who hate guys like him who hurt little kids.
No TV, no videos, no games, no books, no friends—he shouldn't have everything he likes. And he should say, 'I'm sorry' to all the children and then go back to jail.

From,
(Child's Name)

The children, their parents, friends and relatives are all victims. Investigators were victims of hate and distrust—hearing comments like "you must be crazy doing this investigation;" and two years later being criticized by the same person for not sharing details of the case during the investigation. The defendants and their families continue to feel victimized, but their healing will begin when they face the truth about the activities of Robert Fulton Kelly, Jr.—the activities that led to the disclosures of the children who attended the Little Rascals Day Care Center.

It is important at this point to learn a few things about the primary victims in this case—the children. Defense attorneys and editorials claimed one cannot rely on children's memories; and they claimed the stories that sound too fantastic to be true are mere fantasy. Consequently, they said that statements concerning sexual abuse should also be discounted as either fantasy or therapist implantation—statements about spaceships, babies in microwave ovens, pirates on boats, old men with blood poured on them in the back of Mr. Bob's plumbing van. Well, you get the picture. Defense attorneys said that there was no rational explanation, so the disclosures should be disregarded along with everything else the children said.

Children have excellent memories—

Example #1: Six months after visiting Santa at the American Legion building, my two-year-old son told me (in words he did not know at eighteen months) that he wanted to go see Santa on the stage at the American Legion. I did not know what he was talking about until I was reminded that his grandparents took him there to see Santa six months earlier. Many of the disclosures to the parents in the Little Rascals case were just as innocently unsolicited. One child allegedly told his father when he was paying for gas with a credit card that Mr. Bob used a "magic key" like that. Children stated that Bob Kelly threatened to kill their parents and showed them he could use his magic key to get into their homes.

Example #2: My son told me at age three he wanted to see the caboose at the historic site we visited one year earlier. I could not remember the caboose until I went there and saw it for myself. Children can remember very well—usually at times adults consider inconvenient.

Children also have strange descriptions of real events or real feelings. A child who will not go to sleep because tigers are under his bed has some kind of fear. It may be something significant or a typical childhood anxiety. Whatever it is, the tigers under the bed are just as real to the child as the anxiety diagnosis might be to a Ph.D.

At age four, my son told neighbors, "My mommy eats blood." My wife filled in the details. She had four wisdom teeth pulled that day and was spitting blood.

While traveling past a white wooden church in another county, my son exclaimed, "I went to that church." After ten minutes of questioning, he gave a detailed description of the people there, the drawings with the feathers, and other information. My wife and I knew he had not attended this church. Finally, my wife remembered she and our son attended a wedding at a white wooden church elsewhere, eight months earlier, when he was only three years old. The details were accurate. The feathered drawing was the guest register at the entrance.

It is important to try to understand what the child is saying or the basis behind his or her comments.

On a visit to the pediatrician's office at age six, my son told the doctor that he could not remember what he wanted for Christmas, even though all he ever talked about was "Power Rangers." Also he conveniently changed the time frame on his daily tummy ache. He told the pediatrician that it happened at 9 A.M. after arriving at school, not before school. Since he disagreed on my earlier discussions that his stomach aches were related to not wanting to go to school, he did not want the doctor to make the same conclusion. He had always complained prior to leaving home but then told his teacher at school he was fine.

The doctor's conclusion was that the transition was the problem—it was not a school phobia; but the conclusion may have been different if the real facts had not been known.

A child saying "I don't know" when he or she does know is common. Rearranging facts for some goal or purpose is also a skill learned very early in life.

In another case, a child nearly five years old shouted, "everyone is naked; they're really, really naked." The child was grinning and was an avid viewer of the Ray Stevens commercial where Stevens shouts, "Are you naked?" Realizing the child was obtaining the reaction he wanted, the mother waited until the next day to question the truth of his statement. He admitted he was just teasing.

Robert Kelly's home was described by children as a building that could "walk." It was located seven miles from the Little Rascals Day Care Center in a group of trees hidden off the main highway. The home was built near the water on stilts. Were they fantasizing or expressing their view of a house on stilts?

The children in this case gave some strange descriptions, and Kelly is perhaps the most appropriate adult to explain, but he maintains nothing happened. The children also gave some explicit descriptions that could only be interpreted as sexual abuse of children. Only firsthand experience can explain what is described in the following excerpts of some of the "Bill of Particulars" issued prior to Kelly's trial.

"Bill of Particular" excerpts with names omitted or substituted with parenthetical descriptions. The time, date and place was described in each case according to the period of time in which the child attended the center. Note: "a bill of particulars" is considered a set of allegations until guilt or innocence is determined in court.

- "An unidentified adult male put his penis into the mouth of the victim while the defendant was taking pictures."

- "The victim was forced to perform cunnilingus on an unidentified female. The defendant was taking pictures."

- "(A defendant) performed fellatio on (the defendant) while on her knees in the presence of the victim."

- "(The defendant) inserted his finger in the vaginal opening of the victim."

- "The defendant put his penis into the mouth of the victim."

- "The defendant raped the victim while at the New Little Rascals Day Care Center. It hurt and the victim bled some. This occurred upstairs and (a defendant) cleaned up the victim."

- "The defendant put his finger in the anal opening of the victim in the presence of an unidentified black man during naptime at the Old Day Care."

- "The defendant committed a crime against nature with (an adult person) in the presence of (a victim). (An adult person) put his penis into the defendant's mouth and squirted stuff down the defendant's face. The stuff was white and runny. Then the defendant put his penis in (the person's) mouth. The defendant got angry and (the person) left."

- "The defendant put his penis into the mouth of the victim while at the New Little Rascals Day Care Center. The stuff that came out was white in color."

- "(A defendant) engaged in fellatio with the defendant in the presence of (a victim)."

- "The defendant had no clothes on, took his wee-wee and squeezed it on himself in the presence of (a victim) while at the Old Little Rascals Day Care Center."

- "The defendant put his finger into the anal opening of the victim while at the New Little Rascals Day Care Center. It felt terrible and she told him to stop.

- "The defendant put his finger into the anal opening of the victim at the New Day Care Center at naptime."

- "The defendant engaged in sexual conduct with (a defendant) in the presence of (a victim)."

CONCLUSION: The domino theory accurately describes the victimizing effects of child sexual abuse. The dominoes can stop falling, but only through the healing process that rebuilds and restores the trust destroyed by the victimization. Therefore, therapists should be consulted as early as possible when a child is victimized.

The national media should have been more careful about some aspects of its research and coverage. Several correspondents in magazine articles and television programs may feel they projected a balanced view, but ninety-five percent of the letters from the public across this nation resemble the comments at the end of this book. They view Robert Kelly as the victim and the children and their parents as the perpetrators.

Justice has placed Kelly in prison. Some misinformed journalists have unjustly imprisoned the parents and their children within the walls of negative public opinion.

It is clear who the victims are—the children. Consequently, it is important to destroy the myths concerning the abilities of children so they may begin to heal.

Myth—Children have bad memories. False, they have excellent memories, and it is best not to forget that.

Myth—Children always fantasize. False, children describe real events and real feelings in ways adults fail to understand. It is difficult to fantasize about something you do not know. Children disclosing the sexual acts described in the Little Rascals case were not verbally or cognitively capable of making up such fantasies.

Myth—Children could have made those disclosures by hearing it from therapists and other children. False, my son watched the news many nights during Kelly's nine-month trial because his grandfather served as Kelly's deputy escort to the courthouse. He has not made any allegations about "Mr. Bob." Anyone who believes the Little Rascals children's disclosures about Robert Kelly are contrived is very mistaken.

Myth—Children who make latent disclosures do so as a result of therapist manipulation. False, disclosures made at a later date are common among sexually abused children. If a therapist purposely falsifies documentation or creates false impressions affecting a client's mental recollections, proper investigations should be conducted concerning these alleged activities.

An eight-year-old child wrote a letter about sexual abuse one year after leaving a foster home. The very cordial and well-liked foster parent took a lie detector test to prove innocence. After failing the test and breaking out in tearful sorrow, a complete and detailed confession was given. Public opinion would have cried fowl if this child's latent disclosure challenged the adult in a court of law without the confession.

This is also a good example of my positive disposition towards using a polygraph as an investigative tool. Several of my most difficult cases were solved when the perpetrator confessed in light of a polygraph examination.

THE PERPETRATOR—People do not as children say, "Gee I want to be a heroin addict when I grow up!" Nor do they aspire to be a pedophile, a perpetrator of sex crimes against children. However, like becoming a heroin addict, it can happen to anyone. The following are some general characteristics a perpetrator may develop over time.

The perpetrator:

A. Is usually well-known by the child.

B. Likely victimized as a child.

C. Is a master manipulator.

D. Makes adamant denial.

E. Fails at rehabilitation.

F. May gain either sexual gratification or sadistic satisfaction from the abuse. The sadistic satisfaction allows the abuser to cope with his or her loss of control when he or she was abused as a child. This is a power game for the perpetrator.

G. Has favorite age groups.

H. Loves children and would do anything he or she could for a child and, therefore, cannot understand why they have been accused of doing anything wrong.

Many perpetrators have extremely bizarre ideas for gaining satisfaction from their sexual exploits. Much of the excitement and satisfaction is derived from the planning, manipulating and commission of sexual crimes and the subsequent cover-up. Sexual intercourse is not the sole element the perpetrator needs to satisfy his or her needs.

A child molester may or may not need the use of drugs or alcohol; but many times addictions tend to be multiple in nature; and "drugs and alcohol" often serve as a partner due to their non-inhibiting capabilities. Drugs and alcohol serve as a justification to the perpetrator for either not remembering what happened or for losing control. Many child molesters do not use intoxicants but probably suffer from some type of dual addiction.

Perpetrators of sex crimes tend to have codependent relationships. These are relationships that help them successfully continue their sexual abuse activities. Listed are four cases of codependent relationships that are virtually impossible to believe, but they are based on fact.

CASE #1—The perpetrator admits to sexually assaulting his/her fifteen-year-old child. The spouse kicks the child out and begs the spouse to remain in the home with him/her and the other nine-year-old child. What are the chances for this nine-year-old child?

CASE #2—The perpetrator confesses to sexual intercourse with the son and the daughter and later tells the spouse the confession is not true. The spouse believes the perpetrator's second recollection and alienates the children—considering them to be liars.

CASE #3—The perpetrator returns from prison "rehabilitated," and the spouse who is now a grandparent leaves the five-year-old grandchild in his/her care. In his/her case, five-year-old children were always the favorite age group. What do you think happened to this child? You are absolutely correct!

CASE #4—The spouse caught her fourteen-year-old child and the perpetrator naked in the woodshed. She knew something must be wrong but just could not quite pinpoint the problem until the child disclosed two years later what had happened. Hallelujah! The spouse kicked the perpetrator out—at least for a while.

Remember the denial issue? Even in the situation where a perpetrator confesses to the crime, the codependent may continue to deny the abuse. (Note: Some perpetrators have even been known to report themselves.) This is the reason so many victims also face denial issues. It is obvious that the children do not have a chance. The odds favor the perpetrators when support is needed, and the most vulnerable segment of the population suffers further humiliation and loss of trust.

There are two very dangerous people involved in many child molestations—the perpetrator, directly, and the codependent, indirectly.

What about children molesting children? This is a major occurrence in the "battlefields." Child-on-child abuse is a serious problem, but I maintain it's part of the trickle down theory. Somewhere up the line, there is a lifetime child molester plying his or her trade. Remember the domino effect.

Our society unfortunately promotes the idea that it is okay to forcefully or manipulatively impose the will of one person upon another. Adults cannot continue to stand back and say, "it's just kids exploring." Child development is not something one should learn from the back of a cereal box; and sex from the walls of a toilet stall. Americans need to wake up and realize children need proper care and appropriate developmental nurturing if they are going to lead emotionally stable and happy lives.

The subject of sex in this society is considered "taboo" and it is the "taboo" that has fostered a plush hunting ground for sex offenders and the environment for teen pregnancies in this country for more than two hundred years. (Compare birth dates with marriage dates on available records from the 1700s and 1800s. One will find plenty of out-of-wedlock teen pregnancies during those periods commonly thought of as "puritanical times.")

"Denial" is the key word for this lesson. It is the basis for understanding every issue surrounding child sexual abuse. Examine this set of conversations and begin to understand the denial problem.

Conversation #1: "Do you think they really abused those children. Well, forget it. I just don't want to talk about it. Boy, how about that Jeffrey Dahmer thing. They ought to go ahead and send him to the electric chair."

"Yes, I face this sexual abuse issue everyday. I really do think..."

"Hey, forget it—I don't want to talk about that stuff. I'm going home and check out the news on this Dahmer guy and see how many people he had for dinner—ha! ha! ha!"

Conversation #2: "Well, if he did abuse those children, I hope they get him good in prison. In fact, I would support the death penalty if it weren't for the fact they could put some innocent guy to death."

"I thought you were a death penalty supporter."

"Yeah, but I could not support it for child sexual abuse. An innocent guy might be fried."

CONCLUSION: Denial is a problem with perpetrators, codependents and victims; but as demonstrated above, it is an intrinsic problem throughout our modern society when dealing with child sexual abuse issues.

People would rather read about and discuss serial murder than face the reality of the epidemic dilemma thousands of children face everyday. They are afraid many innocent people might be sent to prison falsely accused of child sexual abuse, yet consider the convictions of other types of criminals as solid cases.

If the denial is not confronted and erased from the face of this nation, the disease will continue to reap its devastating effect. Ignoring cancer does not make it go away. The conviction of Robert Fulton Kelly, Jr. demonstrated twelve jurors could overcome this anchored denial and face the horrifying reality of Mr. Kelly's actions. Three jurors later demonstrated the strength of the denial factor by saying they had misgivings about their verdict. Nonetheless, convicted felons like Mr. Kelly often face their own horrifying reality as evidenced by the following anonymous letter from inmates at Harnett County Correctional Institute which was made public shortly before Kelly's trial.

The following is a letter sent to Robert Kelly, late summer 1991, allegedly from inmates at Harnett County Institute where North Carolina's child sex offender program is located. Script resembles original handwriting.

Dear Mr. Bob,

Those of us already in the system are waiting to greet you with open arms—among other things. Throughout the state, we are well informed of what it is you have done and we are looking forward to working with you, to help you fully understand the nature of your charges. We are very anxious to help you overcome such tendencies: Because some of us are victims of child abuse ourselves, we are able to relate to your problem. When we learned of how you stuck pens, pencils, and fingers up little boy's and girl's rectums, we became extremely alerted to this, for it is something that goes on quite often around here—except for the use of pens, pencils, and fingers. The food, as with other aspects of our living conditions, leaves a lot to be desired; but you can make it Mr. Bob. There's nothing to be afraid of in here—Mr. Bob. The gang and I will look out for you.

Sincerely,
Spanky & The Chain Gang
H.C.I. Home of the "Big Rascals"

THE INVESTIGATOR—There is one major difference between criminal investigations and The Department of Social Services (DSS) investigations. The DSS has one major responsibility—to determine the need for child protective services (CPS), as it relates to a primary caregiver. Law enforcement handles non-caregiver cases and criminal investigations of substantiated Social Services CPS cases. To determine CPS, a social worker must investigate the circumstances and either substantiate the allegations or "unsubstantiate" them.

When allegations are unsubstantiated the case is closed. When allegations are substantiated the case requires a protective services plan. When the goals of the plan are met, the case is closed. Evidence of sexual or physical abuse must be reported to the District Attorney's office. The DA determines the need for a criminal investigation. The criminal investigation by law enforcement gathers evidence for the possible indictment and prosecution of the suspect by the prosecutor. State and/or local authorities may be involved at the DA's direction.

A recent legislative change now requires DSS to directly notify the State Bureau of Investigation (SBI) within twenty-four hours of receiving a report of sexual abuse at a day care facility. This new law is similar to the law requiring notification to the DA since he is the chief law enforcement official. The primary difference is the pressure it adds to the State Bureau of Investigation. Hopefully, the legislature will back up the new law with the funding needed to support these additional responsibilities of the highly professional SBI force in North Carolina. This legislative change was sponsored by a relative of a child who attended the Little Rascals Day Care Center.

Many investigations have been flawed in other areas of the country because each investigative agency has different mandates and these agencies often work against each other. This is not true in Chowan County. I am proud of the cooperative nature of agencies. It has provided protection for children in the county and it was a major element in the successful investigation in the Little Rascals case.

One major drawback in the Little Rascals investigation was the delay in acquiring search warrants. If search warrants could have been issued much earlier, there may have been more physical evidence, especially evidence relating to pornography, which would have clarified the allegations concerning pornography. A list of typical materials used by pedophiles may be used for the warrant when evidence suggests pedophile activity.

In an investigation of potential sexual abuse, one of the best sources of information is the alleged perpetrator. Treat him or her professionally and with good manners. Work just as hard to clear the perpetrator as you do finding evidence against him or her. The perpetrator will provide you with a wealth of information. As I learned with Little Rascals, an alleged perpetrator may give an excuse or an explanation containing information that could only be known by the person that committed the crime.

The most important thing to remember when investigating disclosures by children under the age of six is that there is some basis for their information. It is the investigator's job to determine the meaning of the disclosure—to understand the basis for a child's statements. The child understands his motivation or reason for his disclosure, but he may be unable to convey this important information to the investigator. Consequently, the investigator must determine whether the child has seen, heard or experienced the event he or she is disclosing.

Possible tools to determine the facts of the case include polygraphs, psychologicals and colposcopic medical examinations. A child's false accusation against an adult may not be a lie, but may be the result of wrong identification or a complete misunderstanding by well-meaning adults. The investigator's goal is to determine the truth of the matter because this is the only way the child can be adequately protected.

I told my wife on the first night of the 1994 South Carolina Susan Smith case that a polygraph would send investigators in the correct direction. Unfortunately, that direction left the nation stunned. However, it also left us a little more aware of the importance of having these knowledgeable, trained professionals in the field of child investigations.

CONCLUSION: The Department of Social Services must determine the need for protection for a child by investigating allegations involving a primary caregiver. A protection plan is established when the allegations are substantiated by DSS. Law enforcement is responsible for obtaining evidence for the DA who prepares a case for possible prosecution and is also responsible for investigating allegations of abuse involving non-caregivers.

The system works better when agencies cooperate—especially in team investigations. Investigators of child sexual abuse tend to burn out early. Team investigations greatly help in the reduction of the stress levels involved.

Better pay would also help reduce a lot of stress and assure quality in frontline workers. Some counties have advertised CPS positions paying as low as $14,500 per year. Many law enforcement officers put their lives on the line daily for similar near-poverty-level pay scales. What society pays its athletes and what it pays for the safety and protection of its children is an indictment of criminal negligence. The penalties may be too great to pay if change does not soon take place.

The following letter written by Dr. Robert F. Perry shows the importance of cooperative relationships between agencies. Dr. Perry has worked with, among others, Dr. Thomas Noguchi, M.D., who performed the autopsies on Marilyn Monroe and Robert Kennedy. Dr. Perry's work with Dr. Noguchi in teaching resident physicians about the responsibilities of health care providers to recognize and report suspected child abuse cases demonstrates his acute awareness of the problems and controversies that surround this most serious of crimes.

August 10, 1993

David McCall
Edenton, NC 27932

Dear David,

It has certainly been my pleasure working with you these past months in your role as investigator for Child Protective Services. We have witnessed a number of tragedies as we each serve as advocates for the children—and, somewhat sadly, it is our shared interest in abused children that has brought us together as colleagues.

Even with the ever-increasing awareness by the medical community of the 'Battered Child Syndrome,' this societal anomaly of infant and child abuse still, too often, goes unrecognized by otherwise competent and caring health care providers.

Unquestionably, the principle reason for 'missing' this diagnosis is the apparent reticence of many to even consider the possibility of nonaccidental injury in their differential assessment. Given that violent crimes against children occur with frightening regularity throughout all socioeconomic strata, acute physician/nurse/etc., awareness of the signs and symptoms of child abuse seems essential to the protection of these entirely helpless victims. Recognition and active intervention must therefore become the 'gold standard' of care for all practitioners involved with the medical treatment of pediatric patients.

Your book, David, brings this message to the forefront and teaches that we must, at all times, consider the possibility of caretaker abuse whenever we are confronted with a physically or emotionally traumatized child.

I thank you for sharing this text with me. It is a topic that deserves our attention and our advocacy. Please do not hesitate to call upon me if I can be of service. Until then, accept my warmest regards.

Sincerely and cordially yours,
Robert F. Perry, M.D.
Department of Pediatrics
East Carolina University School of Medicine
Pitt County Memorial Hospital

CRIME TIMELIME:
The Little Rascals Case

This case is central to my frontline experience. Its size and complexity, as well as the involvement of so many people, make it an experience unequaled in the world of child sexual abuse investigations. While it is not necessarily the most unusual sexual abuse case I have investigated, its size and publicity are two parameters that make it different. These two factors demand that we learn some kind of lesson from the largest and most expensive child sexual abuse case in North Carolina history. The following chronology and outline highlight the details of this important case.

CHRONOLOGY OF ALLEGED EVENTS

July 1986—Bob and Betsy Kelly purchase and begin operating the Little Rascals Day Care Center on Court Street in Edenton, North Carolina.

September 1988—The center is relocated in a renovated Double Cola Bottling plant one block away on East Eden Street in order to expand the business by accommodating more children.

January 1989—The Chowan County Department of Social Services receives a child sexual abuse allegation against Bob Kelly and begins its investigation and later substantiates the allegation.

February 1989—The DSS investigation is completed and the District Attorney authorizes an investigation by the Edenton Police Department. The State Bureau of Investigation (SBI) dispatches officers to assist in the investigation at a later date. The Child Day Care Licensing Section conducts its investigation.

March 1989—Child Day Care Section substantiates allegations. However, there are discussions about not revoking the license. Further consultations result in a revocation of the license. (see appendix)

April 1989—Bob Kelly is charged with sexual abuse of three children. The center does not close until the end of April, after charges are lodged and children of the many parents who remained loyal to the Kellys begin to make disclosures.

Summer 1989—Several SBI agents are assigned to interview workers from the day care center. William P. Hart is assigned as a special prosecutor from the State Attorney General's office to assist H. P. Williams, the District Attorney. Assistant District Attorney Nancy Lamb is assigned to a case which has similar disclosures as those made in Little Rascals. This case is later tied to the Little Rascals case and Lamb assists in Robert Kelly's prosecution. Law enforcement and DSS conduct investigations into this other case as indicated in later court records.

September 1989—Elizabeth "Betsy" Kelly, Willard Scott Privott, Kathryn Dawn Wilson and one other defendant are indicted in the Little Rascals case.

January 1990—Two other female defendants are indicted in the Little Rascals case. One year after Robert Kelly sends his child to live in California, sources state that this child guessed six of the seven defendants and allegedly stated he did not want to see anyone get hurt. Also, during Dawn Wilson's trial, prosecutors presented letters she wrote to this minor child which the prosecution claimed were sexually provocative. The letters were mailed in early 1990 when defendants assumed they would soon go to trial together.

February 1990—Judge J. Bradford Tillery, Jr. orders defendants to be joined for trial. Prosecutors fight this action.

September 1990—North Carolina Supreme court overturns Tillery's joinder and allows the prosecutor to separate the trials.

October 1990—Judge D. Marsh McLelland is appointed to the case after Judge Tillery resigns citing case complexities.

December 1990—Change of venue moves Bob Kelly's trial to Farmville, North Carolina, seventy-six miles from Edenton.

April 1991—Trial postponed. Defense attorneys request materials prosecutors say they either already possess or are not allowed under discovery statutes. Judge quashes subpoenas issued by defense attorneys Michael Spivey and Jeffrey Miller. Prosecutors considered the subpoenas to be burdensome and written for the purpose of intimidation. The Judge agrees. The attorneys later ask for that decision to be reviewed. It is upheld by the Appeals Court. This postpones the trial date for June 3 to July 22, 1991.

May 1991—PBS television program about the Little Rascals case airs called "Innocence Lost." As a result, the town's local paper, its citizens and its political representatives receive hate mail from around the country alleging a "witch-hunt" of the defendants in the case.

July 22, 1991—Prosecutors reduce charges from 248 counts involving twenty-nine children to 183 counts involving twenty-two children. Jury selection starts.

August 19, 1991—Opening arguments and the start of prosecution testimony.

October—November 1991—Betsy Kelly is freed on a lowered bond. A former Social Services Board Chairman provides part of the bond. There are headlines about a Montana porn raid connected to the Little Rascals case. It does not play a role in Kelly's prosecution.

December 10, 1991—The prosecution rests its case. Charges are narrowed to ninety-seven involving twelve children.

January 6, 1992—The Defense starts presenting its case.

February 11, 1992—Kelly testifies, "I never touched a child in a sexual way." Sources state his adult daughter wants to testify against Kelly about her own alleged victimization by him.

March 4, 1992—Defense rests.

March 11 and 12, 1992—Robert Kelly's ex-wife, Kelli De Sante, testifies in rebuttal testimony for the prosecution that Kelly received child pornography in a secret mailbox, was obsessed with pornography and even requested her to send soiled underwear to him after their divorce.

March 23, 1992—Closing arguments start. Judge has reinstated three charges bringing the total to 100.

March 31, 1992—Deliberations by the seven-female, five-male jury begin.

April 22, 1992—Robert Fulton Kelly, Jr. is found guilty of ninety-nine charges and sentenced the next day to twelve life terms—one for each child. Authorities say after hearing that Kelly turned down plea bargains when initially charged on three children, prisoners at Central Prison felt he was unjustly convicted and consequently, his transition into the system was much smoother than expected.

November 2, 1992—Jury selection is scheduled to begin in the case of Dawn Wilson, former cook at Little Rascals.

January 26, 1993—Dawn Wilson is convicted and sentenced to one life term. Later in 1993, she is placed on bond to give birth to a child conceived around the time of the trial.

Summer 1993—Prosecutor appeals decision by judge to agree to Betsy Kelly's request to hold her trial in Edenton.

January 21, 1994—Betsy Kelly is judged guilty on twenty-nine of thirty charges when she enters a plea of "no contest." She receives a seven-year sentence. She previously served more than two years awaiting trial and is released from prison on November 28,1994.

June 16, 1994—Scott Privott enters a plea of "no contest" to thirty-seven charges. He receives a seven-year sentence and a ten-year sentence. With time served, he is placed on five-years of probation with five years suspended.

January 9, 1995—Appeals for Robert Kelly and Dawn Wilson.

April 1995—Three defendants still await trial.

May 2, 1995—NC Court of Appeals grants new trials to Dawn Wilson and Robert Kelly. The NC Supreme Court can reverse that decision. If not, there will be a new trial, a plea bargain, or dropped charges.

OUTLINE OF ALLEGED EVENTS

Beginning January 1989

I. According to public court records, a child tells its mother that "Mr. Bob likes to play with little boys' ding dongs and hineys."

A. She asks a friend with the Edenton Police about the child's recent reluctance concerning Little Rascals and his disclosures.

B. A report is made to the Chowan County Department of Social Services on Thursday, January 19, 1989.

II. Career Social Worker Grenda Coston and Social Worker David McCall expedite a child protective services investigation, spending many sixteen-hour days during the fourteen-day investigation.

A. Police are invited to participate in the investigation in order to reduce the number of interviews for the child. Officer Brenda Toppin (who had attended much of the same training as Social Workers Coston and McCall and conducted previous joint investigations with Social Services) is assigned to the case.

B. Consultation with state CPS officials is maintained and Officer Toppin and Social Worker McCall continue to obtain corroborating evidence related to the initial child interview by Toppin and Coston. Two and one half years later, the testimony by children in court is consistent with their early disclosures to investigators who did not provide any leading information or questions that could possibly be used to fabricate the disclosures against Kelly.

C. The investigation is conducted as quickly and as efficiently as possible to prevent potential rumor and gossip from polluting the data being gathered. Corroborating statements concerning abuse in the earliest stages of the investigation are confirmed. Concern that more than one child may be involved is heightened. Social Services completes its role with a case decision to substantiate, a protection plan and closure on February 1, 1989. Law enforcement continues its role to gather evidence for prosecution. By March, the Child Day Care Section completes its investigation and makes its substantiation known in its public letter—which was supposed to be posted for public view if the center remained open. (see appendix)

D. Only three or four families are initially supportive of the investigation. The Kellys maintain solid support from many parents for three months. The town newspaper does not run a story for three months until Kelly's indictment. On days five through nine, Bob Kelly greets parents at the center to tell them he has been accused of child sexual abuse. He is not able to give details because he is not provided details. While this accelerates comment and speculation—mostly in support of Bob Kelly—it does not pollute the forensic investigation since specific information is kept confidential.

III. Victims are sent to therapists as soon as possible to help them begin to cope with their victimization. More children begin to disclose information to parents and therapists. The information is given to the district attorney. No further reports on the Little Rascals Day Care Center are made to the Department of Social Services.

IV. Many charges are eventually brought against Kelly and six other defendants in the case based on the district attorney's investigation and further disclosures by the children. While children mentioned other people the DA does not consider suspects, the prosecution feels corroborating statements being made to therapists concerning these other six defendants is sufficient for bringing charges.

V. Robert Kelly allegedly fails a polygraph examination. No one else has claimed to have taken or passed a polygraph.

Beginning September 1989

VI. During this period of other indictments, rumors spread about many local people being involved. The district attorney asks for a stop to the implicating rumors. These speculations appear to subside.

VII. A Little Rascals defendant (prior to indictment in the Little Rascals case) and her fiancee are indicted for allegedly sexually molesting her four-year-old child, following an investigation by the Chowan County Department of Social Services and the Chowan County Sheriff's Department. Though not initially connected, later events allegedly connect the two cases.

A. Allegedly, a relative states in public that although this child did not attend the Little Rascals center, he recognized children from the center and they recognized him even though they supposedly had never met. The child also gave stories consistent with those involved in the Little Rascals case.

B. Allegedly, his disclosure of knowledge about Robert Kelly and Scott Privott came innocently after a visit to the

Chowan County Sheriff's Department jail. The next day he blurted out that he rode on a boat with the big man at the jail—identifying Kelly and Privott as participants in the boat ride.

Beginning January 1990

VIII. The McMartin preschool trial of Raymond Buckey and his mother dominates the headlines.

A. The McMartin case is considered to be poorly handled by prosecutors and handled well by the defense attorneys.

B. Prosecutors and defense attorneys involved in the Little Rascals case make separate trips to California to learn from the McMartin trial. Lessons learned include:

1. It is better to limit the number of charges in multi- victim, multi-perpetrator cases. Focus on your strongest evidence.

2. It is better to separate the defendants for trial.

3. It is best to involve the many agencies and professionals in a cooperative effort from the investigation to the trial.

4. Keep specifics confidential during the course of the investigation.

5. Creating additional evidence such as videotapes of interviews may be used by defense attorneys to win their cases. Using the tapes, the attorney can make the best interview of a child appear contrived. However, the use of videotaping may also enhance the investigative process and satisfy public opinion. (The Rodney King ver-

dict is a good example. If charges were brought, without the tape's existence, and defendants were separated, an initial conviction of some of the police officers involved may have occurred.)

IX. Judge Bradford Tillery honors unprecedented requests by defense attorneys to join trials together. His decision is later overturned by the North Carolina Supreme Court and he steps down. Sources implied that Tillery was a good friend of a father of one of the defense attorneys. However, other sources stated Judge Tillery was conscientiously studying the case and seeking to handle it in a way that he felt would meet the best interests of everyone involved—including the children and their families.

X. Prosecutors and defense attorneys argue over discovery issues. The defense attorneys want all records of all children. Prosecutors contend they are only required to provide what they are going to enter into evidence. Judge J. Marsh McLelland comes out of retirement and does an excellent job handling these issues and others.

Beginning July 22, 1991-Bob Kelly goes to trial. While few if any of Kelly's family from 100 miles south attend, a number of defendants and their families show up to support him during the nine-month trial.

XI. Most of the national press portrays the Little Rascals case as a witch-hunt, but the trial shows this was not the case. This results in a lot of unjustified negative publicity for the town.

XII. An affidavit is taken from an adult who very reluctantly comes forward to say she saw a videotape of a defendant dressed like a pirate on a boat with children. It was in her ex-husband's possession several years ago. Little Rascal's children had made similar disclosures. This results in the "Montana raid." Allegedly, a suspected boat sunk off the NC Coast.

Teen child pornography was found in the raid, according to court records. It was unrelated to any of the victims in the Little Rascals case, however. Two half brothers of the target in the Montana raid served prison terms for child molestation.

In 1993 a twenty-five year old alleges to me that he or she saw a nude Polaroid photo of this individual at a neighbor's house in 1979 at age eleven. This person said, "He was holding a chain saw and a chain and he had a 'hard on,' and I haven't ever seen anything else like that in my twenty-five years."

Other pornographic Polaroids also allegedly exist, but they do not involve children. Some claim it is mere coincidence. Others see developments of this nature as support of the children's disclosures and the idea that the Little Rascals case was likely tied to pornography.

XIII. The testimony of the children in court is just as strong and powerful and consistent as it was during the early stages of the investigation before children went to therapists.

XIV. The physical evidence is disputed by defense experts as being too little and inconclusive. Prosecution experts testify that physical evidence is often not present with victims of molestation; however in this case there is significant physical evidence. Later interviews with the primary examiners find they continue to stand by their exams which they say involved some of the worst physical trauma they have ever seen.

XV. The expert witnesses for the defense attorneys describe exactly the same principles involved in the investigations but try to portray they were not used. Brenda Toppin is unjustly criticized for destroying tapes when she testified she reused tapes of victims after they were properly transcribed.

A videotape of a counselor's interview is shown during the trial, but it does not convince the jury that the children's disclosures are contrived. Also, audiotapes by a primary counselor are available, but the defense chooses not to enter them into evidence.

The expert witnesses do not impress the jury. Some witnesses for Kelly do poorly on the stand. Kelly allegedly contradicts himself by saying he did not transport the children in his plumbing van (except for his own child, niece and nephew) and then saying he did transport children in the van for a period when his car was broken down. A reporter is asked why no one reported this contradiction in the press coverage. He said it was not significant. A juror after the trial said it showed her Kelly was not telling the truth.

XVI. Prosecutors fight the entering into evidence of a test called a "penile plethysmograph" that shows Kelly is not a pedophile—someone who is sexually attracted to children. Since it has not reached the Supreme Court and has not been ruled inadmissible like the lie detector test, the judge has the right to decide. The test results are allowed. Prosecutors realize this loss is actually a win, however, because it allows them to be able to enter Bob Kelly's ex-wife's damaging testimony for rebuttal. The reporters in the newsroom refer to it as the "peter meter," but not in their news articles, of course.

XVII. My own examination of public opinion finds swings from feelings of guilty during media coverage of the prosecution to feelings of innocence during coverage of the defense case to feelings of guilty after prosecution rebuttal.

A. Public opinion after the verdict? Remember the word denial.

B. There are those who know Bob Kelly is guilty—the children, the parents, the jurors, and one must wonder, Bob Kelly. The public says either "well, something might have happened," or "that poor innocent man." Denial sure is an appropriate word for public opinion.

XVIII. The most important evidence presented during the trial was the testimony of the eyewitnesses—the children. Testifying in court can actually be a healing process because the child regains trust by taking control of the situation and confronting the perpetrator. The juror can hear the same horrible disclosures investigators, therapists and parents had to listen to for three years and make up his or her own mind about innocence or guilt. An insurance company for the center settled a million dollar civil law suit in favor of the children in 1994.

Beginning April 22, 1992

XIX. After Kelly's conviction and sentencing to twelve life terms, the children jeer him as he leaves for Central Prison in Raleigh, North Carolina. It was purely spontaneous when a child asked, "Can I tell Mr. Bob something?" and then shouted, "I hate you." The "lamb hunters" blame the parents for allowing their children to do something that is part of the healing process. Interestingly, there was no complaint about the curses cast by family members at Jeffrey Dahmer following his conviction for destroying so many lives.

XX. Special Prosecutor Bill Hart and Assistant DA Nancy Lamb continue to work on the Little Rascals case.

CONCLUSION: The most important thing to remember about this case is that Robert Fulton Kelly, Jr. was found guilty of sex offense crimes against the children who attended the Little Rascals Day Care Center.

I have summarized the evidence presented against Bob Kelly with the following montage of testimony given by the twelve children who testified at his trial. I thank Sheila Turnage, a journalist who is preparing a detailed account of the trial and case, for providing the notes used to develop this summary. Prosecution expert witnesses considered the physical evidence to be consistent with children's disclosures while defense expert witnesses considered the physical evidence to be insufficient. That left the burden of the evidence on the eyewitnesses—the children. Decide what conclusion any investigator, therapist or jury member would have to reach concerning the allegations in this landmark case.

"It made me feel very bad."

"He just told me 'you suck my ding-dong.'"

Child testifies Bob made her lick his penis, and she saw Bob and Dawn having sex.

"He touched my number two with his finger." "On the inside and the outside."

Mr. Bob put his penis "in my mouth." "It tasted nasty."

Child testifies white and yellow stuff came out of his penis. Prosecutor asks, "How did it taste?"

"I don't know because I spit it out." Testified Bob threatened to kill her family.

Child testifies Bob made him put his penis in Bob's mouth and Bob put his penis in the child's mouth at naptime.

"Stuck his finger in my bottom." "Made me feel bad."

Child testifies about being forced to abuse another child. "She done the same thing to me."

Other child corroborates testimony. "He was going to kill me."

Child testified about seeing Bob and Dawn having sex, pictures being taken, Bob using the bathroom in her mouth and he raped her.

"It felt bad."

"Mr. Bob did the touching."

"He peed in it."

"It went in me."

"It just touched me."

One important point needs to be clarified, however. The negative media publicity and Bob Kelly's defense hinged on one major accusation by the Kelly's—that a parent (name withheld), whose son was allegedly slapped by Bob Kelly five months before the DSS investigation, instigated the whole Little Rascals affair. The evidence during Kelly's trial showed this was not true.

The parent kept this incident quiet until another parent, concerned about her child's discussions and behaviors surrounding Little Rascals, asked the first parent how her son was doing at Little Rascals. The second parent did not know the first parent's son was slapped and had stopped attending the center several months earlier. If DSS had received information about the first parent's child, it would have investigated. That information was not discovered until after the DSS investigation began. In fact, it is interesting that the Kellys appeared willing to admit during the trial that Bob slapped the first parent's child. In 1989, those allegations were allegedly denied according to a taped police interview with Betsy Kelly played during Robert Kelly's trial.

Principals in the Little Rascals Case

THE JUDGE—D. Marsh McLelland, age seventy-one. Retired Superior Court Judge and University of North Carolina Law School graduate. Presided over Robert Fulton Kelly, Jr.'s trial and Kathryn Dawn Wilson's trial.

THE PROSECUTORS—Special Deputy Attorney General William P. Hart, age thirty-nine, from New York state, graduated from Duke Law School in Durham, North Carolina.

District Attorney H. P. Williams, Jr., age forty-two graduated from the University of Richmond Law School and was born and raised in Northeastern North Carolina.

Assistant District Attorney Nancy B. Lamb, age thirty-six, originally from Troy, North Carolina is a graduate of Wake Forest Law School.

DEFENSE ATTORNEYS—For Robert Kelly included Michael Spivey, age forty, from Tarboro, North Carolina, a Campbell University Law School graduate; and Jeffrey Miller, age forty-one, who graduated from the University of Miami Law School and now practices in Greenville, North Carolina.

THE DEFENDANTS—The following includes initial charges and court decisions and other alleged identifying information. Defendants not named are those where no final disposition of the case has yet occurred.

Robert Fulton Kelly, Jr., age forty-one in 1989, called "Mr. Bob" by the Little Rascals children, co-owned and operated the Little Rascals Day Care Center. Kelly was convicted on ninety-nine counts of sexual abuse involving twelve children and was sentenced to twelve consecutive life terms in prison. Kelly continued to maintain his innocence after entering prison. Home being Fayetteville, North Carolina, Kelly moved to Edenton in 1974 to serve as the Chowan County Country Club Golf Professional. Charged on 248 counts with 114 indictments and 113 incidents before trial. Attorneys: Michael Spivey and Jeffrey Miller.

Elizabeth Twiddy Kelly, called "Miss Betsy," age thirty-four, co-owned and operated Little Rascals with her husband Robert Kelly. She was also charged in the case. She and Robert Kelly were married in the late 1970s after his divorce from his first wife. Originally from Edenton, her parents continue to live and serve as highly respected individuals in the judicial system and construction industry in Edenton. Originally charged on forty-eight counts involving twenty-nine indictments and twenty-eight incidents. She pleaded "no contest" to some of the charges in 1994. Attorney: Joseph Cheshire from Raleigh, North Carolina.

Willard Scott Privott, age forty. Adopted son of a deceased Judge, Privott worked as a video store/shoe repair shop owner at the time of his arrest. Privott spent more than three years in the Chowan County Jail under more than one-million-dollar bond before going to trial. The state contends Privott's defense did not seek a lowering of bond and caused delays in the trial. Privott maintained his innocence and contended he was being presumed guilty until proven innocent. While defense witnesses, including the Kellys, in the first two trials testified to a social relationship between Privott and Kelly, Privott allegedly stated, "We didn't really even do much socializing, Bob and I." Originally charged on sixty-eight counts involving thirty-eight indictments and thirty-seven incidents, he pleaded "no contest" to some of the charges in 1994. Attorney: John Halstead, Jr. of Elizabeth City, North Carolina.

Kathryn Dawn Wilson, age twenty-three, was convicted on January 26, 1993 of one count of first-degree sexual offense and four counts of taking indecent liberties with children. The second defendant to go to trial, Wilson was sentenced to serve one life term at Women's Prison in Raleigh, North Carolina. Wilson served as the "cook" at the center and had previously served as a day care instructor at a facility in Charlotte, North Carolina. She was originally charged on twenty-five counts with seventeen indictments and sixteen incidents. Her attorney was Edward B. "Bo" Simmons of Tarboro.

Unnamed Defendant, age thirty-four, charged in the Little Rascals case was able to post bond weeks after her arrest with the help of friends and family. She taught four-year-old children at the center. Fourteen charges with ten indictments involving nine incidents were originally made in 1989. No disposition on the charges as of April 1995. Attorney: Frank Ballance of Warrenton, North Carolina.

Unnamed Defendant, age eighteen, was arrested and charged in the case. She worked at the center for less than a year before it closed. Originally charged on twenty-three counts involving fourteen indictments and thirteen incidents. No disposition of the charges as of April 1995. Attorney: Jeffrey Miller.

Unnamed Defendant, age twenty-seven, was the seventh defendant charged in the Little Rascals case with three charges and two incidents. She did not work at the center, but allegedly had her checkbook stolen by Dawn Wilson while Wilson visited in her home prior to the Little Rascals investigation. No disposition of the charges as of April 1995.

LET THE STARS SHINE
CELEBRITY CHILD ADVOCATES

Celebrities carry a great deal of influence in our society. To help the public stand up and listen, I asked child advocate stars for feedback on the production of this book. The following are not endorsements of my book. Rather they are responses I received when I asked for input concerning child abuse and neglect.

I met with Martin Sheen who was visiting friends involved with the Plowshares movement. He expressed his concern for a safer world for all people, including children. Jane Seymour contacted "Child Help USA" and asked them to assist me with my work.

Dr. Ruth called me at home and advised that she would let me know if she located any information pertinent to my work. When we met later, she confirmed the seriousness of the subject, but was unable to provide any further comment.

Oprah Winfrey provided me with a list of resources and explained that one should not face abuse alone. An executive assistant at the Tom and Roseanne Arnold Foundation wished me luck saying every word is important for fighting child abuse. And, Gary Trudeau dropped a note in the mail to suggest where I might be able to locate an agent to help in the publication of this book.

In addition, First Lady Hillary Clinton wrote a one-page letter describing the importance of responding to the needs of children and families. Saying the work sounded important, she emphasized the need to end child abuse and to provide a home where children receive love and proper care. She confirmed her concern when we met shortly before the election.

Marilyn Van Derbur Atler, 1958 Miss America, and Gloria
Steinem, author and women's advocate, were also very helpful.
They provided the following material, with written permission
to publish, to explain their insights concerning child abuse and
neglect.
The following is a letter from Marilyn Van Derbur Atler,
1958 Miss America. The Motivational Institute, Inc. 195 South
Dahlia Street, Denver, Colorado, 80222. Written contribution
by the author.

DEAR SURVIVOR

Dear Survivor, Therapist, Support person,
On May 8, 1992, it will have been one year since I first
spoke the words, "My name is Marilyn Van Derbur Atler. I am
an incest survivor."
On May 20, 1992, it will have been a year since I realized
that finally, at age fifty-three, I felt no shame. NO SHAME!
Why did it take me so long to realize that it wasn't my fault...that
I didn't do anything wrong. Why did I hate, with all my being,
my "nightchild?" She was a precious little girl trying to survive
being used for a big man's pleasures.
Too many people still say, "It happened a long time ago.
Let it go. Get on with your life." The fact that they cannot
believe why we carry the shame, why we feel so guilty, unlov-
able, ugly, and unacceptable only underscores how little is
understood about what happens to a child's mind when his/her
body is invaded and violated.
If you are still locked into the horrific shame, if you are still
suffering from the emotional and physical traumas of your
violative childhood, I say to you, THE PAIN ENDS! I promise
you. If...you do your work! The work of healing can be done
now or it can be done later but the work must be done. There

are no short cuts. No surgeon can open us up and remove the shame and the pain. Only in the speaking of it does our healing begin.

If your violator is still living, PROTECT YOUR CHILDREN. We now KNOW that an adult who violates children almost always violates more than one child and, too often, the children of the next generation. NEVER leave a child with the violator.

Please do not compare your violations by saying, "I was ONLY fondled" or "It only happened for a few months." A child who is violated ONCE can be traumatized at the time as a child, and as an adult survivor.

Broaden your support base. If you are only turning to a "significant other" and a therapist, reach out again. The burden is too overwhelming for the support person. Be in touch with other survivors. Write. Read. Go to support group meetings. Speak of it. Speak of it again. And again. It is your work.

If you choose to confront your violator, don't expect to be validated. Many/most violators BLATANTLY deny any violations. If you choose to confront the one who should have protected you, don't expect, "I am so very, very sorry. Why wasn't I there to protect you? I swear to God, if I had my life to live over again, I would protect you with my life!" If the adult didn't protect you as a child, it is unlikely that the adult will take responsibility for it now. When I finally told my mother, in deep despair, sobbing uncontrollably, she said, "I don't believe you. It's in your fantasy."

For those of you who are engulfed in pain, I wish I could bring you into the glorious world I now live in...I have such peace...calm...quiet. There were so many months when I thought I was losing my mind, when I thought I couldn't hang on one more day. The pain ended. I have found peace.

I hold the precious, innocent child you were in my heart. Marilyn.

"Alas, for those who never sing but die with all their music in them"—Oliver Wendell Holmes—

The following is an excerpt from © Gloria Steinem's book, *Revolution from Within*, NY: Little Brown, 1992. Reprinted by permission of the author.

AN INNER CHILD OF THE PAST

Until recently, I thought I had built a brick wall between myself and my childhood. I valued those early years for making me an optimist (nothing could ever be that bad again) and a survivor (learning how to cope has its advantages). Then I put their memories and feelings behind me.

Of course, I did notice that small things made me feel irrationally sad or depressed—for instance, any story about a mother and daughter on their own, certain landscapes, or the sound of a radio in an empty room—but I just avoided them. When bigger things made me feel self-pitying but defiant—feeling rootless and proud of it, for example, or giving money away but then feeling deprived—I assumed they were the inevitable results of my conscious, rational decisions to remain free, unencumbered, with no possessions to possess me.

I continued in this way for decades while pressures grew. I worked for a magazine I loved and a movement that had given me life. I organized and traveled and lectured; I campaigned and raised contributions and solicited ads to keep the magazine going; I turned my apartment into a closet where I changed clothes and dumped papers into cardboard boxes; and I only once in twenty years spent an entire week without getting on a plane. But at home or away, I often woke up with sweaty palms and pounding heart, worried that I was going to mess up some public event, fail to find enough money to pay the printer and meet the payroll, or otherwise let down this movement that meant as much to me as it did to millions of other women.

After the first five or six years, I had become aware that I was usually doing over again things I already knew how to do and often saying things I'd said before—that I was reacting more than acting—but I also knew that no matter what happened, I could always keep on functioning. It was part of my survivor's skills, my childhood defiance. If there had been an Olympic team for just functioning, I would have been on it. Later, as economic times got tougher for magazines in general and ours in particular, and inevitable backlashes greeted women's advances, I felt pressure to do more and more. When my friends asked about my state of mind or emotions, I made them laugh—and despair—by turning Plato on his head. "The examined life," I explained, "is not worth living."

Then one evening after a lecture on the road, a woman in the audience recommended a book, *Your Inner Child of the Past*. She described it with such conviction that I went out and bought it.

Of course, I wasn't interested in self-knowledge, just research—or so I thought. In this case, I needed insight for a book of essays I was writing about Marilyn Monroe, especially about her childhood as Norma Jeane Baker. The author, Hugh Missildine, a child psychiatrist, had identified the most common sins and excesses of childrearing—overindulgence, neglect, perfectionism, sexual abuse, and so on—and then described each one as it manifested itself in later life. Because Marilyn's story of being sexually abused as a little girl had been disbelieved by other biographers, I was looking to Missildine for confirmation of my belief that Marilyn's lifelong inability to value herself as anything other than a sexual being was a classic result of sexual abuse in childhood.

Even more than obvious abuse, however, the hallmark of Marilyn's earliest years had been neglect. Boarded out as a baby by a mother with severe emotional problems of her own, Marilyn had been so neglected that as a little girl, she believed she was invisible. When her mother was committed to a state mental institution, Marilyn was sent to an orphanage. Only the early maturing of her body and the attention it attracted made her feel "visible" and convinced her that she did indeed exist. It was this division between an internal, worthless self and an external, sexually valuable self that would haunt her for the rest of her short life. Missildine's text described some of the typical results of the kind of neglect Marilyn had experienced: a lifelong search for nurturing, wanting to belong yet feeling a perpetual outsider, trying to make fathers out of husbands and lovers, using sex to get child-like warmth and approval, and neglecting one's own welfare because neglect feels familiar, like home. These were all problems Marilyn herself described. As Missildine wrote: "Many such people, particularly women, are drawn into theatrical and movie work because...'When you're a nobody, the only way to be anybody is to be somebody else.'" It was almost as if he had met Marilyn Monroe; certainly, she had said almost exactly those words.

Such extremes of childhood neglect—and of response in adulthood to that neglect—were clearly Marilyn's, not my own. I read them feeling interested and safe. But soon, this slender, simple little book was describing more ordinary results of neglect—among those with alcoholic, ill, or absent parents, for example—that gave me a jolt of recognition. "The childhood of persons who suffered from neglect," wrote Missildine in his matter-of-fact way, "usually reveals a father who somehow wasn't a father and a mother who somehow wasn't a mother."

Well, my mother had suffered spells of depression, delusions, and long periods as an invalid both before and after I was born. My father had taken care of her until I was ten or so and seemed old enough to replace him. Then my parents separated, and my mother and I lived on our own. Though my parents always made me know that they loved me, and treated me as well as or better than they treated themselves—all very different from the degree of neglect Marilyn had suffered—they still hadn't been able to be real parents much of the time. Basics like regular school attendance, clean clothes, a bedtime, enough money to pay bills, and, after I was ten, any kind of consistent parenting at all, had gone the way of my father's wandering lifestyle. After their divorce, my mother's frequent depressions and need for a caretaker had reversed our roles. Since I always knew they were doing the best they could, I didn't allow myself to be angry—and thus just buried my feelings about what I had missed.

For the first time, I began to wonder what was behind the wall between me and my childhood, and if it hadn't seeped into the present in spite of all my bricks and mortar.

I remembered longing to escape the littered, depressing, rat-infested house where I lived alone with my mother; yet I had recreated an upscale, less dramatic version of it in my own apartment with cardboard boxes, stacks of papers, and long absences.

I remembered worrying as a child about our lack of money and my father's penchant for borrowing it; yet I had saved nothing of what I earned, couldn't resist giving money away, never planned for the future, and often ended up with a familiar feeling of being neglected, deprived, and insecure.

I remembered feeling sad about navigating life by myself, working after school, worrying about my mother, who was sometimes too removed from reality to know where she was, or who I was, and concealing these shameful family secrets from my friends; yet I had chosen to work by myself as a freelancer, and then to do a parallel kind of caretaking for a magazine and a movement. Now as then I turned away sympathy with jokes and a survivor's pride. In both cases, I was turning away from a well of neediness that I feared would swallow me up if I admitted it.

The parallels were so obvious that even I began to see that I was repeating the painful, familiar patterns of home. In spite of my insistence that I'd put the past behind me, that free will and the realities in which I found myself were the only shapers of my life, it just wasn't so.

I began to follow clues backward. Why was the sound of a radio so depressing, though television and records were not? Because the radio had been the only sound in the house where I lived with my mother. Why couldn't I give myself security and a pleasant place to live? Because they hadn't been given to me as a child. Why didn't I ask for help from people who would have freely given it? Because they hadn't been there in the past. Why had I lived my life so that I would be ready to leave anyplace at any time, even if I didn't actually do it? Because that was the way I had protected myself against getting attached to places as a vagabond child.

It may be obvious that we continue to treat ourselves the way we were treated as children, but I lived a diverse and seemingly aware life for more than forty years without figuring it out. I suspect many other people have, too. Only becoming conscious of old and unchosen patterns allows us to change them, and even so, change, no matter how much for the better, still feels cold and lonely at first—as if we were out there on the edge of the universe with the wind whistling past our ears—because it doesn't feel like home. Old patterns, no matter how negative and painful they may be, have an incredible magnetic power—because they do feel like home.

This repetition begins to diminish the moment we're aware of its source, and the more we heal the past so we can respond to the present. As the twelve-step Alcoholics Anonymous-type programs say, "Dig it out or act it out." Though we may repeat some sequence of events and feelings in different ways before they gradually dissolve, at least now the point of power is no longer in others who made decisions for us, but in ourselves.

I don't know whether Marilyn made connections between past and present or not: between her lost father and the "fathers" she kept marrying; between the invisible child she once was and her imprisonment in a very visible image that Hollywood had concocted. Perhaps the patterns went too deep, or perhaps there was too much reward for not changing in a world that paid and praised her for staying helpless and childlike. She died before feminism made clear that women have every human possibility, and even before people like Missildine were beginning to write about the inner child. Whether she could have become strong enough to go back and be a parent to her own sad child of the past, we'll never know. But her life story has helped others, if not herself. Certainly, her often repeated plea to be taken seriously reached out to me, made me want to write about her, and thus gave me the great gift of seeing the echoes of her life in my own.

Each of us had an inner child of the past living within us. Those who needed to build no walls have access to that child's creativity and spontaneity. Those who had to leave this crucial core behind can tear down the walls, see what the child needed but didn't have, and begin to provide it now. The more we do this, the more we know that we are worth it.

And that we always were.

IS THERE JUSTICE?

Many letters received complained about North Carolina justice being a failure due to the Little Rascals convictions. I questioned the justice in other high profile cases. Polly Klass died because allegedly a three-time felon walked the streets. The McMartin preschool case cost more than 10 million dollars before acquittal. And, a previously convicted child molester was shot dead before he had his time in court on the new charges.

Little or no punishment was handed out in the Rodney King and Reginald Denny cases, even though everything appeared to be on videotape. The Menendez brothers admitted to killing their parents, and each received mistrials. Michael Jackson allegedly settled claims of improper conduct with a child with a multi-million-dollar lawsuit settlement. And, O. J. Simpson hired a team of courtroom professionals the average American would not be able to afford.

I guess some versions of "justice" would demand that felons who are serving jail sentences in North Carolina for hurting children be set free and be given an Academy Award for their performances for the media!

How has the system changed to protect children? Does it protect those falsely accused? Is justice being served? How are the rights of the victim and the rights of the innocent protected in today's court?

After a documentary aired in the late 1970s concerning the failure of the foster care system, significant changes in state laws began to take place. The term "reasonable efforts" became the motto of a juvenile court system and child protective services system that considered the removal of children from high-risk situations to be less effective than making "reasonable efforts" to fix the problems in the home.

Social workers became wary of the ability of the courts to support them in their efforts to protect children, and the lack of community resources restricted the successful "fixing" of high-risk abuse and neglect situations.

As society became more aware of what constituted abuse and neglect and the reports greatly increased in the 1980s, the child protective services system and the judicial system became overwhelmed with finding solutions to problems that were always present, but were merely hidden behind closed doors in past generations.

A significant increase in reports included the sexual abuse of children. A judicial system designed to protect innocent adults from being falsely accused was failing to convict guilty perpetrators. The only witnesses were usually the children and the adult perpetrators whom they trusted.

Consequently, state legislatures made some changes in the "hearsay" rules to allow jurors to hear details of abuse that a child might have given spontaneously to an adult listener or a therapist as support of the child's testimony in court.

While many observers feel this violates the rights of the defendants, others find it to be a necessary requirement in order to obtain the truth in these cases; and to see the balance of justice work for children as well as adults.

Debra Whitcomb has produced an excellent body of work addressing most of the recent developments concerning the issues surrounding child sexual abuse and the judicial system. The publication, *When the Victim Is a Child*, Second Edition. Washington D.C.: National Institute of Justice, 1992 is a free publication offered by the United States Department of Justice to help professionals dealing with this issue. Points of view from that document are those of the author and do not necessarily represent any official position or policy of the U.S. Department of Justice. Whitcomb is Senior Research Associate at the Education Development Center, Inc., Newton, Massachusetts. The following excerpts represent some of the issues addressed in that publication.

What is the Criminal Justice Response to Child Abuse?

"Do child sexual abuse cases, many of which involve intrafamilial offenders, belong in the criminal justice system? Opponents of criminal justice intervention point to the system's insensitivity to family needs and particularly those of the child victim; supporters speak of the need to take sexual abuse allegations seriously, not only to exact retribution on behalf of society, but also to validate the victim's position and to shift the blame where it belongs: with the perpetrator." (p.10)

The Risk of False Allegations. "A recent spate of highly publicized sexual abuse allegations has caused the public to recoil and question the limits of credulity. These allegations tend to fall into two categories: sexual abuse of preschool children in day care facilities, sometimes including bizarre and ritualistic elements; and sexual abuse allegations arising in the context of divorce, custody, or visitation disputes. Such cases have caused many observers to question the veracity of child sexual abuse reports...In fact, sexual abuse allegations arising from divorce and custody disputes appear to be quite rare...Research also suggests that sexual abuse in day care is no more common than it is within families." (pp. 6-7)

Why Child Victims Are Different. "Common sense and formal research would agree that children are not merely miniature adults. We know, for example, that children develop in stages during which they acquire capacities for new functions and understanding. We do not, generally speaking, read Shakespeare to a two year old, nor do we expect adult commentary on political issues. Adults, for the most part, attempt to speak to and treat children in accordance with their capabilities. We do not ordinarily expect children to understand or function on a par with adults." (p. 15)

Interviewing Children. In this chapter, Whitcomb discusses three areas of concern with current sexual crime investigations—using anatomically correct dolls, leading questions and videotaping. While the use of dolls and leading questions are considered acceptable in the courtroom, defense experts have criticized their use in forensic investigations. Under certain conditions, however, these tools can be considered to be useful and accurate in conducting a thorough forensic investigation. A current approach tested at the University of California at Los Angeles helps obtain more information without an increase of inaccurate information. The three techniques involved: 1-Rapport building, 2-Instructing the child that one can say, "I don't know," or "I don't understand" and 3-Employing cognitive techniques of memory recall (example: recalling events in reverse order). Whitcomb pointed out in some limited studies involving severe interviewer bias using leading questions, the factual information given by children remained accurate, although the interpretation of those facts did reflect the interviewer bias. She says, "A great deal has been learned in recent years about effective ways to interview children. We have learned, for example, that anyone who questions children about the possibility of having been sexually abused is a potential witness in a court case; this knowledge, gained largely through experience, has encouraged many mental health practitioners, in particular, to acquaint themselves with investigative

techniques that are acceptable to the criminal justice system."
(pp. 33-44)

Statutory and Procedural Reforms. "Public outrage and
intense media coverage of child sexual abuse have prompted a
flurry of proposals for reform in the way child protection and
criminal justice systems handle these cases...In sum, there has
been a tremendous amount of activity targeted at the perceived
needs of child sexual abuse victims in the context of criminal
proceedings. Yet many of the proposed innovations and reforms remain controversial." (pp. 47-52)

Competency of Child Witnesses. "As we have seen, studies
suggest that on most tasks inherent in testifying, children have
sufficient skills to testify. A relationship between age and
honesty has never been shown, and it may be fair to say that
young children cannot independently fabricate truly credible
descriptions of events outside of their experience." (p. 62)

Alternatives to the Traditional Courtroom. "The Supreme
Court's ruling in Maryland v. Craig offers hope for prosecuting
cases in which child victims are threatened or intimidated by the
defendant's presence. In striking a balance between protecting
children and preserving the right of confrontation, the Court
recognized that unless alternative means of testifying can be
accommodated under certain circumstances, many young children will be effectively precluded from testifying, some cases
will never be prosecuted, others will be dismissed, and justice
will not be served. Nonetheless, it remains likely that prosecutors will continue to view videotape and closed-circuit television
as 'last resort' measures when all other efforts to obtain children's testimony have failed." (p. 81)

Statutory Exceptions to Hearsay. "In cases of child sexual
abuse, the child's out-of-court statements may be the most
compelling evidence available. Indeed, hearsay may be the
only evidence, since child sexual abuse frequently occurs in the

absence of other witnesses or physical trauma to the child, and the child may be found incompetent or otherwise unavailable as a witness...The states have shown great interest in special statutory hearsay exceptions to accommodate casual, unprovoked disclosures that are sometimes made by child sexual abuse victims." (pp. 85, 99)

Restrictions on Public Access. "There is, to date, no empirical support for contentions that children are traumatized by the presence of an audience during their testimony. Anecdotal evidence suggests that the courtroom audience is not a concern for many children. To be sure, some children will indeed be humiliated by public exposure of their victimization. In such cases, courtroom spectators generally comply if the prosecutor asks them to leave...As a matter of policy, the media should respect the private dignity of these children by withholding any identifying information and by refraining from exploiting the potentially sensational nature of these crimes." (p. 109)

Use of Expert Witnesses. "Among the most disturbing trends in the prosecution of child sexual abuse cases is the increasing reliance on expert witnesses—particularly experts in the behavioral sciences—by both the prosecution and the defense...As a final observation, it is worth noting that placing appropriate controls on the use of expert witnesses is well within the discretion of the trial court. Careful consideration of the expert's credentials and the nature and timing of the anticipated testimony ensures a reasoned decision-making process that is likely to be upheld at the appellate level." (pp.111, 120)

The Victim Advocate. "In more than 7,000 communities throughout the United States, child victims are offered support from victim/witness assistance programs." (Information supplied by the National Organization for Victim Assistance, Washington, D.C., September 19, 1989.) "In the juvenile court, where most allegations of child abuse and neglect are adjudicated, child victims typically have a guardian ad litem (GAL) appointed by the court to represent their best interests. Appointment of a GAL is mandated under the Child Abuse Prevention and Treatment Act of 1974 for states wishing to receive federal funds." (Child Abuse Prevention and Treatment Act, P.L. 93-247, 1974)

Streamlining the Adjudication Process. "Among the most frustrating aspects of our criminal justice system are (1) the need for witnesses to repeat their stories over and over again, and (2) the length of the adjudication process...Given the nature of the American justice system, there is probably some minimum number of interviews to which every witness, including children, must submit. Similarly, there often are perfectly justifiable reasons for delay. These facts may seem intuitively obvious to an adult, but to a child they may be puzzling, at best, or even overwhelming. Though there are ways to streamline the adjudication process, all depend on some level of cooperation among the agencies involved—a quality that cannot be legislated or mandated. Instead, it must come about through the joint efforts of some very committed people." (pp. 135, 144)

Conclusions and Recommendations. "It is important to recognize...that much of what has been learned through experience and research on sexually abused children should be applied to every child who is a victim of, or witness to, a crime. Certainly, any of the courtroom reforms can be just as beneficial to child witnesses of parental homicide, for example, or to child victims of kidnapping or other traumatic crimes, as they are to child victims of sexual abuse. Similarly, improvements in investigation and intervention, particularly in the area of case management and coordination, can be equally helpful to child victims of any form of parental maltreatment. Likewise, counseling or therapy should be an essential element of case planning for every abused or neglected child, since research suggests that all forms of childhood victimization can have serious repercussions in later life." (p. 154)

Many people believe the judicial system in the United States has severe flaws that prevent it from finding "justice" in cases involving children alleged to be abused or neglected. Some believe the laws do not go far enough to protect children. Others believe the laws do not serve the principle of "innocent until proven guilty." Both sides of the issue contend the ones who ultimately suffer are the children; and improvements in the system must be made.

There is justice in the system; but like any system, it can always be improved. Whitcomb's professional work concerning the current judicial issues that relate to child victims helps to provide some very important insights.

Kimberly A. Crnich, a survivor, is a lawyer and co-author of the book: *Shifting The Burden Of Truth: Suing Child Sexual Abusers—A legal Guide for Survivors and Their Supporters*, available through Recollex Publishing, Dept. V, 333 S. State St., Suite 326, Lake Oswego, OR 97034. She offers an alternative to criminal prosecution. Taking civil action is one means of finding justice for the victim. The following summary is excerpted in part from the book. The information in this summary does not constitute the giving of legal advice. Please check with competent professionals for advice regarding your specific circumstances, as factual differences and local laws will cause individual case procedures and results to vary considerably.

THE DECISION TO SUE
By Kimberly A. Crnich, J.D.

Summary

No reason to sue is more right than another. A survivor may be angry because of the high cost of therapy and want reimbursement. Trial strategy in this situation would probably focus on maximizing financial recovery, which may mean being willing to settle out of court before trial, to reduce attorney fees. A survivor may be eager to have a public confrontation of the abuser in a trial, with a determination of liability by a jury. In such situations, a survivor may be unwilling to settle out of court. It is crucial for a survivor to understand the personal reasons for pursuing a lawsuit so the litigation can be structured to get the best results.

The process of contacting a lawyer and inquiring about rights, even if the survivor decides not to go forward with the case, may meet the survivor's needs. Some survivors have found merely contacting a lawyer very empowering. This may be the first time that someone in a position of legal authority recognizes that the survivor has been wronged and informs the survivor of his or her legal rights against the abuser. Merely having the knowledge that the legal system, and by extension society itself, is recognizing and acknowledging that survivors have, and should have, legal rights against their perpetrators can be tremendously empowering.

TRUTH AND DENIAL

As I heard testimony at two of the Little Rascals trials, I began to realize a great deal of truth could be found in denial. Defense witnesses testified a child was bitten on the cheek allegedly leaving eight to ten teeth marks, but denied any wrongdoing. Another defense witness testified Kelly and a female child came out of a bathroom and the child was crying. This allegedly was explained away as a discipline situation.

Another witness denied ever being abused by Kelly while admitting Kelly had broken a boat paddle across his body. Another defense witness remembers her own daughter saying Kelly did things to little boys that he should not do. There is a lot of truth in the denial; and truth is the commodity a good investigator desires to possess.

Another good example of denial on the level of the judiciary is found in a case not connected to the Little Rascals case. In this case, a judge would not allow as evidence photos of a severely bruised and battered child, since the photographer was not present in the courtroom. In fact he allegedly refused to view the photos and dismissed the case. The judge's denial placed procedure above "truth."

The following material by Dr. Roland Summit, provides case studies that clarify the issues surrounding "truth and denial."

TOO TERRIBLE TO HEAR
Barriers to Perception of Child Sexual Abuse

By Roland Summit, M.D. © 1987, adapted from a paper written in support of testimony before the U.S. Attorney General's Commission on Pornography, Miami, Florida, November 20, 1985. Dr. Summit is Head Physician, Community Consultation Service and Assistant Clinical Professor of Psychiatry, Harbor-UCLA Medical Center 1000 W. Carson, Torrance, CA 90509. Written contribution made by Dr. Summit.

After some twenty years as a community psychiatrist, with the last ten years focused almost entirely on child sexual exploitation, I have reached some disturbing conclusions about the role of child sexual abuse in American society. I believe that as a people, as a nation and as a collection of child caring institutions we have maintained, like the three monkeys, a self-protective posture of see no evil, hear no evil and speak no evil. Sexual abuse of children, child pornography, with its companion vices of child prostitution and sexual molestation, is explained away, trivialized or simply denied whenever there is a risk of confrontation. While the greatest motivation for denial rests in each of us as adult individuals, our need to deny is bolstered by the relentless irrelevance of protective institutions and the paralyzing, calculated confusion imposed by an unknown number of influential citizens whose private lives are devoted to the sexual subjugation of children. Protective institutions like the family, church, schools, medical and social service agencies, police, courts, government and public media are not irrelevant to most of the needs of children, but all such resources remain devoted to beliefs, policies and priorities that not only ignore but often obscure the impact of adult sexual interest in children.

If there is an enthusiastic traffic in sex with children and if little kids are consumed for the sake of its production, how could such an empire stay in hiding? I would like to reflect on seven dimensions of denial which serve as protective camouflage. That classification is followed by a number of illustrative examples.

DIMENSIONS OF DENIAL

1. **Self-protection:** Every individual is more comfortable believing in a happy childhood and in a just and fair society. Recognition of child sexual exploitation requires the ability to suspect trusted resources, to question one's own judgment and competence in selecting those resources, and to empathize with the terror and helplessness of a child who submits without question or outcry. Belief in sexual exploitation forces a reappraisal of societal trust and a challenge to habitual confidence in protective institutions.

Individuals with untroubled childhoods tend to idealize their memory and resist identification with issues of victimization. The near-majority of adults who as children experienced some level of sexual assault tend to be especially reactive against painful clues to their past. Many who have suppressed all conscious memories of abuse feel unexplainable pain and anger with any reminder. Others experience themselves as bad for attracting abuse or for submitting to perversion. They may despise young victims and defend the needs and motives of the aggressor. Some are still locked into perverse sexual imagery. They protect the right to gratify themselves at the expense of children, or at least to have access to pornographic imagery.

All of us, whatever our niche in that spectrum of victimization experience, will tend to band together as adults to endorse the unchallenged myth that child sexual abuse is practiced only by obviously degenerate strangers on somebody else's child. Even if we see molestation in progress, we will believe it is something else. (See case #3, Big Pine and #7, Miami Vice.) Given a choice between believing in a complaining child or an accused adult, most of us search long and hard for some reasonable explanation that will exonerate the adult. (See #5, Motherly Love.) We shrink from believing even our own children if it means exposing our failures to the community at large. (See case #1, Stranger.) There is a continuing, centuries-old tradition of blaming the victim and of maligning the complaining parent whenever a respectable adult is accused. Any professional who speaks for the child will be targeted also for blame. (See cases #2, #5, #6, #7.)

2. Victim Suppression: We assume that any legitimate crime victim will complain. But sexual abuse of a child is not a legitimate crime, and those who participate are not considered legitimate victims. If a child fails to make immediate outcry, and if a child fails to describe a conventional, recognizable style of crime, then the burden of proof that such crime exists reverts to the child and on any adults credulous enough to support the child's tenuous complaint.

Instead of defining the crime and forging new tools to combat it, we use our distrust of the children to avoid recognition and to resist innovation. At each level of disclosure, from child to parent to authorities to enforcement we are too humiliated with the scandal of the crime even to entrust it to a higher level of scrutiny. (See cases #1, #3, #7.) Most sex crimes involving children are therefore never reported, and most such crimes reported are never charged.

In a large survey of female victims of child sexual assault, two percent of the assaults were reported to the authorities when the offender was a relative. Only six percent of non-related offenders were reported (Russell, D., The Incidence and Prevalence of Intrafamilial and Extrafamilial Sexual Abuse of Female Children. Child Abuse and Neglect. 11983, 7: pp. 133-146).

3. Inadequate Investigation And Evaluation: Control of child sexual exploitation requires ingenious infiltration and intelligence as well as a considerable investment in data management technology. Despite increased sophistication in parts of the system there is not enough coordination to make sense out of the disparate efforts of investigative reporters, governmental commissions, customs and postal inspectors, missing children services and federal, state and local law enforcement agencies. With child pornography, for example, there are thousands of pictures without known children. And there are thousands of photographed children without known pictures. Far from establishing credibility, these two opposing clues tend to nullify one another. Obscene pictures of anonymous children provoke only helplessness, while children who report being photographed in the midst of sexual exploitation trigger a single-minded pursuit of the photographic evidence. The almost inevitable failure to find identifiable photos tends to discredit other aspects of the child's story. Every unproved allegation seems to encourage the hope that nothing the child is saying is true.

Investigation of child exploitation is fundamentally different from other crimes, in that infiltration, stakeouts and covert observation are ethically forbidden. The urgency to protect the victim at risk competes with the need to develop evidence. Also, the first tentative outcropping of a sex ring typically does not invite the kind of effort required for timely search and seizure. Note in the following cases (#5, motherly Love, #6, Bakersfield, and #7, Miami Vice, as well as in notorious allegations like the McMartin preschool and Jordan, Minnesota, cases) that search warrants were applied too late to find the reported pornography. Even when pornography is confiscated (Case #1, Stranger, #3, Big Pine, and #4, Family Business) it will be withheld from public exposure, thereby encouraging trivialization within the community.

4. Adversarial Inhibition: Sex crimes, more than "legitimate" crimes, seem to require criminal conviction to justify public validation. That standard in itself represents another Catch 22 in favor of traditional denial. The insistence of proof beyond reasonable doubt for an invisible and illogical crime almost guarantees suppression and repudiation.

The appropriate defenses against charges of sexual misconduct are "aging the case" and "discrediting the victim." By the time a case is argued through pretrial motions, depositions, preliminary hearings and delayed adjudications, both the children and the public have tried to put the crime away. If child, parent and clinical interviewer can survive the public exposure, leering, scapegoating and assault of endless adversarial examinations, the only lesson for future planning is avoidance. It is little wonder that families avoid reporting. Considering the normal immaturity and confusion of victims, the typically trustworthy style of child molesters, and the predictable adults and ambivalence of jurors (and judges), the reasonable doubt of one adult will cancel the testimony of dozens of children.

The rejection of cases and the in-camera bargaining of pleas create an illusion of unfounded or trivial offenses. Focus on only the chargeable offenses diverts attention from the real dimensions of crimes still only dimly understood. Even if convicted, the narrowly contrived charges of sexual molestation avoid hearsay allegations of studio cameras, drugging, group prostitution, conspiracy and bizarre ritual.

The ultimate obscenity, mutilating and killing a child for the titillation of viewers, has been described by numerous children throughout the country. Descriptions of drinking blood or urine and eating feces are almost routine. (See case #7, Miami Vice.) The suspicion that such atrocities might be staged in a trusted neighborhood preschool is simply intolerable to anyone. The continuing voices of alarm come mainly from the parents who hear these accounts from their three-and four-year-old children.

Such reports, while remarkably consistent from one out-cropping to another have yet to be confirmed by a credible adult eyewitness or by recovery of the photos, movies and videos or the bodies and ritual paraphernalia that the children insist they have seen. Yet the descriptions are so graphic and the scenes are so strikingly similar and the implications of any such reality are so massive that some kind of adult conceptualization is urgent.

In my informal and scattered overview of some twenty-five investigations involving reports of blood ritual, each has be-come hopelessly confused and deadlocked. Investigations are suspended. Charges are contrived to avoid the issue. Witnesses who talk of ritual are dropped from consideration. Many cases are simply never filed because of the inflammatory effects of the unprovable rumors. And those that go to trial may be dropped in midcourse, acquitted or reversed on appeal. Each failed attempt at prosecution buttresses the logical and wel-comes argument that such charges are obviously ridiculous, and that adults who choose to believe them should be viewed with suspicion.

The unhealthy and undefinable relationship among very young children, adult prurience, pornography, ritual and death is one that defies available knowledge and logic. Until there is some better forum for understanding, it would be wise to shield both the children and accused from adversary rhetoric to sus-pend criminal prosecutions and to assign the process of inves-tigation to a more charitable arena.

5. Kill The Messenger: Anyone who participates in un-covering a suspected nest of exploitation may now be accused of coaching witnesses into false accusations. Defense attorneys and a few clinical expert witnesses are claiming that specialist interviews telegraph the interviewer bias to an impressionable child, who will respond with fantasies that are interpreted as real by the crime-seeking specialist. Both claims exploit the fact that most children don't admit to their role in sexual exploitation unless they are reassured and given permission by an experienced specialist. Since child victims are typically trained to be most fearful of telling their parents and since parents may be the most reluctant to imagine that their children are at risk, the child specialist who elicits the first disclosures of abuse will be a very unwelcome messenger. Children who disclose to an empathic interviewer may take back their allegations in the face of dismay from their parents or disbelief from more skeptical examiners.

In a typical pattern of investigation of suspicions of group exploitation, an interviewer may receive convincing denial from all of the children interviewed. In a subsequent round of interviews one child may implicate the children who have continued to deny. The child who breaks the secret, often somewhat older than the others, may claim that he resisted involvement or even fought back against assaults, but that he knows things happened to other kids. With progressive interviews and with increasing reassurance and rapport, the specialist interviewer may pry open this tentative "window of disclosure": "he did it to me too...but only once." "He did it to me a lot of times." "He made me do it to him once...a lot of times." "She did it too." "They all did it." "They made me do it to the other kids." "They killed babies." "They made me kill the baby." Such admissions are rarely volunteered. They are confessed in response to questions that focus on a presumption that such things might be possible. On encountering outrage or disbelief, the admissions will evaporate in reverse order, the more lurid, fearful and self-incriminating yielding to the safer ground of credible acceptance.

A child who is confident with one listener may be mute with someone who is more upset or unbelieving. His mother may believe, while the same stories fill his father with incredulous rage. Similar hierarchical barriers to credibility line the path of disclosure to police officer, prosecutor, media reporter, editor, juror and judge. In general the more authoritative the position and the less time a person spends in the company of children, the less such a person can hear from a victimized child. When several children at different stages of disclosure are interviewed by several adults at different levels of credibility, the apparent paradox divides those adults into polarized, warring positions, with strident, passionate advocacy at one end countered by logical, obstinate rejection at the other (#6, #7).

While this example assumes that each of the children is sharing his own limited version of the truth, such a process of deliberate uncovering by interviewers of different biases invites the suspicion of error. If a child first said no and later said no, who but a fool would reinforce the yes in between? And if only the kindly, reassuring examiners hear the worst news, how can we trust that the children are not simply striving to please the examiners or to impress them with imagined or invented atrocities? Such questions deserve respectful dialogue and patient deliberation.

The rapid emergence of child sexual abuse diagnostic specialists and the predictable challenge from attorneys for the defense have produced a forensic dogfight. People who were hailed a few years ago for their contributions to discovery are now being condemned as self-serving inventors and malicious witch-hunters. The tools that launched the explosive sexual abuse awareness of the past five years—anatomic dolls, figure drawing, improved physical examinations, symptom checklists and patterns of expected victim and perpetrator behavior—are denounced as instruments of abuse. The methods are attacked to invalidate the outcome, and the messengers are destroyed to challenge the message.

Since the collapse of prosecution in the Jordan cases and the bleak report of the Minnesota Attorney General, the position of all prosecutors and therapists involved in abuse investigations has yielded to progressive attacks. Cathleen Morris, the Scott County prosecutor, was held accountable to civil liability for possibly false arrest. She was impeached and nearly removed from office both for being too zealous and too timid in pursuing the charges. Prosecutors with similar cases throughout the country suddenly disowned the fledgling teamwork they had built with child therapists and social service workers. In the Los Angeles County McMartin case, therapists reporting new allegations from alleged victims felt a chilly reception accepted as legitimate flaws by prosecutors who suddenly lost confidence in their clinical experts: overcredulous, cross-germinating, leading, misguided, poorly trained, unscientific. Trauma-specific therapy has fallen into disrepute and disclosures outside of police interrogation have become a liability. Therapists who shared with parents the meaning of their child's nightmares were considered irresponsible with evidence, while children who would not repeat the same stories to official investigators were dismissed as unreliable. These discarded witnesses identified possible linkages with other centers and described shared, pornographic rituals. Information considered not safe for prosecution is then not available to develop some rational comprehension of the many cases as a whole.

As the body of uncharged rumors becomes controversial and seemingly fantastic, the case in court is more vulnerable to defense and media attack. Prosecutors may shift to the defensive and repudiate whomever was responsible for assembling the case. In the McMartin case, still grinding through the eighteenth month of preliminary hearing, both the original prosecutor and her specialist interviewer have been blamed. Kee Mac Farlane, the interviewing social worker, has been pilloried in the courtroom and excoriated in the press. Her playroom techniques and her use of puppets and anatomic dolls have been attacked as child abuse and brainwashing. Throughout the nation specialist interviewers face massive civil suits. Many have retreated to less punishing work.

Just as evidence and testimony seems doomed to evaporate under harsh scrutiny, defense arguments are hard to disclaim. The turning point position of Jordan hinges on the condemning scapegoating of the prosecutor, police investigators and therapists who allegedly conspired to entrap children and to destroy families for their own professional aggrandizement. When those allegations were examined in the Federal Court of Appeals (Eighth Circuit, District of Minnesota, No. 85-5243) the justices found them groundless, endorsing both the motives and the methods of the child advocates. That seasoned, sober review and endorsement came too late to save Cathleen Morris from defeat at the polls. It is also neither timely, newsworthy nor dramatic enough to offset the prejudice that has come to jeopardize public confidence in any similar investigation.

The search for unspoken evidence of sexual abuse goes back to the dawn of modern psychiatry and involves its most revered and controversial pioneers. The painful controversies that have always tainted anyone probing for child sexual abuse help to explain the continuing professional acrimony about what diagnostic techniques can be trusted as accurate and proper. Freud used hypnosis and free association to retrieve forgotten scenes of sexual assault from the early childhood of his original patients. His first clinical paper in 1895 claimed that those forgotten traumas were the cause of hysteria. Some thirty-five years later Freud's favorite student, Sandor Ferenczi, advocated a posture of tenderness and reassurance to "free the tongues" of patients who were afraid to recall and to resolve traumas associated with childhood sexual assault. Ferenczi described lifelong effects of sexual trauma that are only now being rediscovered in research on multiple personality states. While the right to search for underlying sexual trauma is once again at least somewhat legitimate, it was a disastrous notion for both Freud and Ferenczi in their time. Freud was renounced by his teachers and other superiors for daring to suggest that sexual assault was an important problem. Eventually he regained professional respectability by renouncing his sexual trauma theory. He apologized that in his youthful enthusiasm for discovery he didn't realize that the stories of abuse were only fantasies.

In 1933 Ferenczi risked offending Freud by reviving the issue with new clinical data and even stronger conclusions. Ferenczi died a year later in disgrace, alienated from his mentor and dismissed as crazy by his colleagues. His epic paper was assigned to obscurity as nothing but the product of Ferenczi's terminal dementia.

To the present time, those who call attention to the hazards of child molestation and those who develop techniques identifying the signs of sexual abuse have been ridiculed and disgraced. When methods or concepts are sound, people are attacked for their eccentric style or for their inferior credentials. In fighting uphill against entrenched indifference, many of the crusaders developed an urgent stridency. The choice of some to punctuate their message with exhibits of child pornography proved only that audiences would not tolerate the bearer of such an offensive display.

Lloyd Martin gained national attention in the seventies by establishing a Los Angeles Police Department special unit for sexually exploited children. He broke sex rings and lectured tirelessly to small audiences on the dangers of pedophilia. He offended many people with his pictures of semen-drenched infants and his warnings against overzealousness, and he was removed from his post as an embarrassing incompetent. Dr. Ann Burgess, a professor of nursing, published a landmark paper (sexual trauma of children and adolescents: pressure, sex and secrecy, Nursing Clinics of North America 10, pp. 551-563) in 1975 and edited the first major textbook on child sexual assault in 1978. She was awarded a federal grant to study the effect of child pornography and went on to define the nature and effect of sex ring exploitation. Her conference on pornography at Boston University was picketed by the North American Boy Love Association and she was denounced to her employers for her unscientific collusion with police officers and other zealots. More recently she was censored by the board of the Kinsey Institute of Human Sexuality.

Bruce Woodling is a family physician who began correlating sexual victimization with previously unnoticed traces of vaginal and rectal scarring. His lectures and clinical papers have established an unprecedented expertise in diagnosing sexual trauma. Dr. Woodling was called before the California Board of Medical Quality Assurance to defend against charges that his observations were not based on adequate research.

Again and again, those who find ways to recognize child sexual exploitation in the midst of traditional disbelief have been forced to retreat or to suffer continuing attacks on their competence and motivations. Not only does this counterattack paralyze the scapegoated individuals, but it discourages most of those who might otherwise emulate the beleaguered pioneers to establish a continuing, institutional base of knowledge and research.

In the past five years there has been an unprecedented explosion of interest, information and public education in every aspect of child sexual abuse. Adult survivors, children and even perpetrators, all of whom were invisible in the past, have come forward to provide understanding and a more child-protective mentality. It is only since incest awareness has led to a broader concern for children exploited in out-of-home settings that this apparent enlightenment has been dubbed a witch-hunt. And those who uncover hints of conspiracy and of a more sinister fabric of grotesque perversion are the ones who draw the most expensive and well-organized opposition.

The progress of the past five years, the people who have sparked that progress, and the concepts and diagnostic skills that could sustain progress are at risk of being buried under a new avalanche of punishment. The growing ability to recognize and to define the motivations and dimensions of organized exploitation would be suffocated in that avalanche.

6. Deliberate Deception: Most case suppression and system failures can be attributed to unintended denial and chronic public avoidance. That does not preclude the influence of treacherous decision-makers and gatekeepers. A doctor, judge, attorney, police officer, editor, writer, school administrator, teacher or parent can also be an invisible pedophile, pornophile or cultist. Children describing multiple-perpetrator abuse typically implicate trusted institutions and community leaders among the peripheral players. In one case under investigation the site of alleged pornographic production belonged to a physician. Policemen and police vehicles are described in several other cases. A social worker is named among the Bakersfield predators, as well as parents and grandparents (Case #6, Bakersfield). The uncertainty of sorting out enemies from friends impairs the emotional security of victims and their advocates, labeling fearful believers as paranoid or malicious compared to the "normal" majority who find such allegations outrageous.

7. Conceptual Chaos: Each profession in every age has contributed new traditions of avoidance which serve as dogmas of denial. These conservative doctrines are challenged by recent practitioners expounding revisionist beliefs, which in turn inspire logical protests. Unlike other fields of knowledge, awareness of sexual crimes against children has been revolutionary rather than evolutionary and self-contradictory rather than self-evident. There is no reliable standard of proof and not even a scientific nomenclature for most of the phenomena associated with adult sexual interest in children. Until a more seasoned base of knowledge develops the speculations of the investigators will be hopelessly outclassed by the cunning of practitioners. Whatever evolution of concept the last ten years of progress have initialed, those concepts are far too immature to survive another ice age of reactive denial.

Continuing progression defining the motivation, scope and significance of child sexual abuse in this country will require a new commitment to view a wide scope of issues relating to adult victimization of children. Every such issue is offensive to adult comfort and each will tend to fragment constructive alliances. Only an extraordinary effort and a strong sense of coalition can empower us to hear the small voices and to overcome the enormous pain.

CASE EXAMPLES

The following cases represent deceptions between perpetrators and victims as well as confusion of adult perception and intervention. All have been drawn from my professional consultation experience.

Case #1 "She's a Stranger to Me"—A man in Redondo Beach, California, lured preteen girls into his house with ads on market bulletin boards soliciting household help. He was arrested after postal inspectors linked him with commercial promotion of child pornography. Local police identified some fifteen children in the photographs with the help of school authorities. The investigation was stymied when not one of the children's parents would identify their child in those pictures. Although the man was eventually convicted at the federal level of misusing the mail, the problem was never dealt with at the community level. The families involved received no professional help. The community gained no protective awareness or skills.

Despite examples like this to the contrary, clinical experts who repudiate children in court insist that honest, credible victims inform their parents without hesitation, and that parents have no reason to suppress complaints unless the accused is a member of the family.

Case #2 Mr. Peepers—Mr. "Peepers" presented himself to parents in his neighborhood as a commercial photographer. He touted a nonexistent nationwide search for another star to promote a major hamburger chain, using fake credentials. He convinced the parents of eight-year-old "Janie" that she could be a sure winner. They allowed him to take Janie to his studio for a modeling session. Janie was glum but non-complaining upon her return.

When Peepers returned to take her for a second session the next day Janie ran crying to the back of the house and refused to accompany him. After extended conflict and refusals to explain, Janie reluctantly told her mother that Peepers had taken nude photographs and fondled her genitals. Peepers was reported, investigated and tried on felony charges. Defense contended that Janie's failure to complain the first day proved that subsequent charges were contrived. Despite the obvious enticement of the phony contest and false credentials, Peepers was pictured in court as the hapless victim of a frame-up designed by the parents to cover their supposed dealings in narcotics. The choice to report Peepers' assault forced Janie and her parents to endure humiliating punishment and groundless scapegoating in the courtroom.

In reviewing their guilty verdict, several jurors acknowledged that they had discredited Janie's complaint until they heard expert testimony explaining typical reasons for initial silence. Janie's parents vowed never again to risk involvement in the criminal justice system.

Case #3 Big Pine—"Johnny" a nine year old from Los Angeles, complained of a bellyache on the dawn of his second day of school in Big Pine, a very small mountain resort in the eastern Sierras. His mother urged him not to be afraid of his new school. He became more adamant in his refusals to return to school and more desperate in his excuses, until he blurted out an unbelievable story. He said he had been invited by an older boy to join a noontime club and taken to a classroom blindfolded for an initiation that included being stripped, orally raped, and both threatened into silence and invited into continuing participation. Johnny's mother called a relative who was a deputy sheriff based in another community. A covert investigation implicated Mr. "Friendly," who was one of the most trusted and indispensable teachers in the district. He was loved for his remarkable devotion to children, which extended to volunteer coaching and spending weekends taking groups of fifth and sixth grade boys on fishing excursions in his camper.

Mr. Friendly quietly accepted arrest after a search of his classroom cabinets yielded body oil, sexual devices, cameras and large quantities of both still and motion pictures depicting Friendly in oral and anal group sex. These films apparently were shot in his classroom, camper and outdoor campsites. Investigation revealed that Mr. Friendly had initiated into his "club" almost every fifth grade boy in town over the past four years, a suspected total of over a hundred children. He used older members to entice initiates and to establish secrecy. He also used confidential school files to reinforce silence through guilt and fear: "I know your mother has been in a mental hospital. If she found out what you're doing it would put her right back into the booby hatch."

Even though everyone knew everybody's business in this isolated community, there was the typical avoidance of suspecting dear Mr. Friendly as a menace. One father described finding his son in bed with the man when he came to pick him up after a birthday party. It was not the least unusual for Mr. Friendly to help out at any gathering of boys, and the father was embarrassed at his initial alarm. Mr. Friendly explained that he had rescued the boy from a fight and was soothing him in the darkened room with massage.

Police officers sequestered their own sons from questioning. Teachers signed letters of support for Friendly when a defense attorney planted a story that a disgruntled clique of girls had accused their colleague of sexual touching. Three mental health specialists provided independent evaluations to the court. All recommended outpatient counseling and diversion so Friendly could resume his contributions to school and community. One said he had already been punished enough through his expulsion from the volunteer fire brigade. Another promised a cure through sexual therapy for his wife, whom Friendly described as frigid and frustrating. All agreed that the boys were willing participants, and that Friendly constituted an attractive nuisance rather than a menace to the community. Overruling the experts the judge found Friendly to be a mentally disordered sex offender and sentenced him to a closed treatment facility. The community sealed over without a trace of its scandal. A Mental Health Department project to provide confidential, private counseling for the boys died without a single referral. A new high school teacher arriving four years later remarked at the unusual behavior of his eleventh and twelfth grade boys. They reminded him of seventh graders preoccupied with silly bathroom humor and discomfort in close relationships with girls. None of his fellow teachers acknowledged his expressed concern. No one dared to mention the legacy of Mr. Friendly.

Case #4 Family Business—Don Stephenson is a pedophile who expresses sublime delight in his exploits with children and his virtuosity with a camera. Both are recorded in meticulous detail in nine audiocassettes he had dictated to a friend. The tapes were seized during a sweep of what came to be called the international pedophile ring. Since no children are known to have complained about his adventures, Stephenson's incidental arrest allows for the study of a "successful" pedophile, the "well-adjusted" predator who might spend a lifetime molesting children without notice.

In his tapes Stephenson went on for hours about the technical aspects of making and copying stills and movies. He produced pornography for personal pleasure, for trading and for publication. He extolled the beauty and the missionary value of child pornography magazines and dropped names of his friend who published them. He also praised the effort of a physician pen pal who was establishing an orphanage as a front for pornography production and prostitution. He dreamed of the day when pedophiles could achieve liberation like other erotic minorities. He wondered why any father would avoid the pleasures of incest and expressed puzzlement that some of his child-loving friends chose to spare their own offspring. He worried about the prospect of his own daughters outgrowing his taste for juveniles, but consoled himself with the hope that each could conceive by him another child "to serve me into my old age, so to speak."

He illegally adopted his two daughters, "T. and L." in Asia when each was an infant. He trained them from the outset to engage in sex, loving and praising them for their responses. He counseled other pedophiles on the proper initiation to intercourse after some years of lingual and digital dilation of the immature vagina. While he denied ever using force and insisted that a well-prepared girl would passionately desire to be penetrated, he advised seeking a remote location because "there's bound to be a certain amount of noise, and she may have trouble sitting or walking for a few days."

While working in Japan Stephenson employed a young Vietnamese girl as a baby sitter. He soon married her, using her baby-sitting services to attract the young children of U.S. military families. In one such weekend engagement he describes the use of his four-year-old son, "J." and his two daughters to draw another four-year-old child, "Jodie," into pornographic poses. He rhapsodizes about his sexual initiation of Jodie's eighteen-month-old sister, "Ginnie." The next day, after inducing Jodie to suck his penis, he is quite sure they are in love.

As Stephenson finishes this breathless memoir he pauses to joke of the possibility of a knock on his door to signal the return of enlightened and enraged parents. His easy humor reflects the experienced assurance that Jodie will keep her secret without even a word of warning. And, of course Ginnie is too young to speak.

What makes the follow-up of this case noteworthy is not the criminal conviction but the helpless equivocation of the Juvenile Court.

Stephenson argued the right to keep his contraband family together despite his own photos showing both him and his wife in sexual activities with their children and despite the wife's total dependence on his control. A courtroom jammed with seven lawyers (judge, county counsel, and one each for Stephenson, his wife, and the three children) and various clinical experts spent days arguing about the potential merits of family treatment and discrediting any expert opinion that couldn't draw on controlled studies of Vietnamese mothers raising sexually active children in the enforced absence of a dominant American father. The tapes were not admitted into evidence at that hearing because the judge didn't want to suffer through a seventeen-hour audition. Although Stephenson freely acknowledged a lifetime of pedophilic assaults beginning in early adolescence, one psychologist was pleasantly surprised by his claimed avoidance of coercion, calling him "dangerous to society only in a psychological sense." That report recommended keeping the family together to allow participation in a program designed for incest offenders.

The failure of the Juvenile Court to free the children for adoption kept them in a recycling limbo of institutional placement, exposing them to Stephenson's annual appeals to recapture them. The aggressive appeals accused the children's therapists of psychological kidnapping and (having a) financially vested interest in their recommendations for continuing therapy. Although a series of judges held for continuing out-of-home placement, they tended to accede to Stephenson's demands that the children be reevaluated continually by more "objective" clinicians.

Don Stephenson was eventually discharged as untreatable from the prison-based sex offenders program. Therapists decided his passionate obsession indicated a more than fatherly interest in regaining his children. That same legalistic obsession hammering a resolutely objective juvenile court denied the displaced children any hope of permanency, planning and normal family life.

Case #5 Motherly Love—A radio journalist researching a series on sexual abuse discovered clues to suspect that her young cousin, "Julie," might be a victim of sexual abuse. She spent two invited weekends together coaxing twelve-year-old Julie into admitting that her stepfather, "Mr. Jones" was having intercourse with her. Several more discussions brought forth descriptions of years of cruelty and sexual abuse, including Julie's anguished confession that her mother took movies of the assaults.

The ensuing legal battles left both cousins wishing nothing had ever been said. Julie was trapped for months in juvenile hall, while the mother fought to regain custody. Julie quickly retracted claims of her mother's participation, but stuck to her accusations against the stepfather. Mrs. Jones was overheard offering Julie enticements and threats aimed at exonerating her husband. At the same time she presented herself to authorities as determined to divorce the man for the protection of her daughter. Her unblemished reputation as a leader in her church reinforced her posture of innocence.

Julie's emancipated nineteen-year-old brother called her from another state to offer sympathy. He explained he had been humiliated and raped by their stepfather for years and that he decided to leave home when he was forced to have intercourse with his mother while the stepfather made movies of the event. He learned of Julie's involvement only after Jones' arrest, when their mother called to warn him to keep silent about his earlier experiences. When, instead, he flew in to testify at the dependency hearing, his mother was overheard to say, "I was hoping your plane would crash. But you've been dead to me ever since you left home."

The court-ordered psychological evaluation was introduced at the hearing. The psychologist ignored reports of the brother's involvement and focused instead on Julie's unpleasant disposition and her distrustful sarcasm in his interview with her. He found her accusations less credible than the affable denials of the parents. Crucial to his sympathy with the parents was the reasonable alternative they offered to the lurid claims of pornographic exploitation, paraphrased as follows:

"Perhaps we went too far in our attempts to give the children a positive, healthy idea of sex. One time we invited our son to watch us making love. And another time we had Julie feel Jack's penis and see firsthand what sex is all about. They must have misunderstood or remembered it all wrong. Goodness, we can see now what a terrible mistake we made."

The psychologist was both impressed with their candor and appalled by their judgment, giving him hope for the educational counseling he advised to prepare the mother for the return of Julie to her care. Although he discounted Julie's claims of sexual abuse, the hatred of both Julie and her younger brother for their stepfather was so apparent and his cruelty was so well-documented that the psychologist recommended against any attempt at reconciliation with Mr. Jones.

In view of the adult brother's testimony, the judge assigned Julie to the protective custody of other relatives. The parents reunited and earned glowing recommendations for a reunification with Julie from their family counselor. That therapist, a former erotic filmmaker with deceptive clinical credentials, had been suspected of encouraging pedophilic activity as a volunteer in several incest treatment programs. He was also implicated as a pedophilic missionary during police investigation of a school teacher suspected of child molestation.

One of Jone's brothers originally told an investigating officer that Jones had bragged about sexual escapades with his wife and children and that he had projected one of the films to prove it. He later denied the statement. The films were never found.

Case #6 Bakersfield—The city of Bakersfield, 100 miles north of Los Angeles, has reverberated with sensation and scandal ever since the announcement in April 1982 that the parents in two families had been arrested for sharing their children in extended pornographic exploitation.

Alvin and Deborah McCaun were accused of sexually assaulting their two small daughters, as well as melding their daughters in shared sexual activities with the two young sons of another couple, (names withheld). Also accused were Rod Phelps, father of Deborah McCaun, and his wife, Linda, McCaun's stepmother. Charged as accomplices among a larger number of unnamed suspects in group activity were Betty Palko, a social worker, and her aging boyfriend, Larry Walker. They eventually testified that they had been drugged, tied up, photographed in sex acts, whipped and hung from ceiling hooks for sexual purposes.

A hint of the case had surfaced two years earlier when one of the McCaun girls accused her grandfather, Rod Phelps, of molesting her. During that investigation the mother, Deborah, acknowledged that she, too, had been molested by her father as a child. It was apparently during that first exposure that Betty Palko, who had professional knowledge of the case, became enmeshed in the alleged sex ring activities.

The two girls told of their grandfather showing pornographic movies before hanging the children from the ceiling for the enjoyment of assembled guests. They accepted as a routine the "three things:" penetration of their mouths, vagina and anus.

They described their mother's apparently insatiable demands for oral sex. And they talked of cameras used in the home and distant locations. The boys described groups of strangers taking pictures and penetrating their bodies in what sounded like out-of-town hotel rooms.

After removal from home the four children showed great fear of retaliation and complained of relatives harassing and threatening them. Attempts at therapy were abandoned because of defense attorneys claiming discovery of all records. At the trial a police surgeon from London refuted Dr. Woodling's medical examinations describing gross, traumatic enlargement of vaginal and rectal openings. He also claimed that children are led easily into false allegations by persuasive interrogators. The judge refused to qualify rebuttal expert opinion regarding patterns of truthful disclosure. Although some corroborating physical evidence was found, all traces of pornography eluded detection.

Despite withering cross-examination and public disbelief, the jury found for the veracity of the children. The four parents shared a total of 1,000 years of penalties imposed by a judge who pronounced, "these defendants have stolen from their children the most precious of gifts—a child's innocence." At the time of sentencing seven other sex rings were under investigation in this rural, sparsely populated county. Several included allegations of overhead hooks and photography.

Testimony from those investigations led to suspicions of satanic ritual infanticide and cannibalism, resulting in a media showdown ridiculing the sheriff, who believed the children, and endorsing the more sober judgment of the district attorney, who didn't. A much publicized dig for bodies and satanic artifacts was unproductive, destroying the credibility of the sheriff. Another barren excavation was focused on property owned by Rod and Linda Phelps. At this writing (3-13-87) Rod and Linda are fugitives from justice, having jumped bail after their arrests in 1982.

The Bakersfield phenomenon offers chilling parallels to Jordan. The specialist deputy district attorney, who was so effective in the McCaun Trials, was assigned to routine prosecutions, while generalists took on the sexual abuse cases pending. Most of the cases were dismissed. The major newspaper shifted from coverage to attacks on the patent absurdity of the investigations. After a blue-ribbon task force review of the entire scandal, the State Attorney General issued a report echoing the findings of Minnesota: Multiple interviews, inappropriate use of clinical specialists, cross germination, incompetence.

Counselors treating the children say privately they are dealing with the ravages of unbelievable cruelty. Their supervisors, however, assume such stories were implanted by the investigations. They instruct counselors to discredit memories of atrocity and to restore children's trust in the adults they have learned to fear.

Case # 7 Miami Vice—Shortly before Christmas 1983, a baby-sitting service was offered in Country Walk, a newly built, affluent community in suburban Miami. Iliana Fuster offered to care for her neighbors' children in her home on a daily basis or as-needed overnight and weekends. Her husband, Frank, operated a mobile decorating service as well as this cottage industry. For the parents, including many working wives and others involved in setting up their new lifestyles, the Country Walk Baby Sitting Service must have seemed almost too good to be true. By September of 1984, with Frank and Iliana in jail amid stories of mass sexual exploitation and incredible perversion, the emerging truth was too terrible to hear.

During the ensuing investigation the stories got worse: naked games, terrible threats, weird masks and costumes, drugs, urine, feces, blood, slaughter of animals, cameras, videotapes, cycles of painful, humiliating and horrifying sexual interaction among the man, the woman and the children and between child initiators and infant initiates. (For a remarkably gripping, forensic documentary of the Country Walk case, read *Unspeakable Acts* by Jan Hollingsworth, New York: Congdon & Weed, 1986.) One child talked, then three children, seven, fifteen, twenty-seven children. Boys and girls, Frank and Iliana, another man, another young woman. Where was this coming from? Where would it end? When would it stop?

Defense attorneys said it was coming from the system. Police had swept in without reason in late August and had frightened children and all the families into believing the rumors that had emanated from a few fanciful kids and their hysterical parents. Two psychologists, a married couple bonded in a strange affection and eccentric style, took children with no prior complaints into a playroom and assaulted them with leading questions, fearsome suggestions and pornographic dolls until they emerged spouting recitations of sadistic ritual. These same agents of the prosecution told parents to believe their children and to praise them for each new sordid story.

Iliana took a lie detector test which demonstrated conclusively that she had no role in any improprieties with the children. A second polygraph was equally convincing. In both tests there were evasions about Frank's role. But Frank worked away from home. He couldn't have been there for the daytime rituals described by the more imaginative children. And almost nobody believed some of the stories: drowning a bird, stabbing a snake, eating stool. Frank dressed in diapers forcing children to stuff his rectum with pennies. Anyone should know that these are the monsters in the closets of children, these are the normal anal fixations of four year olds. Dr. Joseph and Dr. Laurie

Braga, self-styled child experts, should know better than to put people in jail with the bathroom talk of little kids.

Outside media stayed out. Local media exploited the marvelous polarities of the case: Iliana is not twenty-four, as presented. She is a sixteen-year-old child bride. Frank is an ex-con. Both are Hispanic victims of Anglo resentment. The Braga's are not psychologists. They are scholars in child development. They're working for nothing. They hold hands. Joseph Braga looks funny in a ponytail and a three-piece suit. Why is Laurie's hair so long? Why do they hold hands? Joseph Braga is an impostor. The real Joseph Braga is dead. Maybe this impostor is a child molester. Joseph Braga is alive and well and living in Miami. Sex. Sadism. Style. Sham. Sensation.

Reflective journalists echoed the misgivings of child psychiatrists and clinical psychologists. If toddlers really went through these atrocities during the day, why would they not tell their parents at night? and what kind of parent would not recognize the unspoken signs of such trauma? Why aren't these Braga people more aware of the influences of dysfunctional parents on impressionable children? Don't they recognize the hysterical fears parents have absorbed from California and Minnesota? Experienced child therapists would understand such things.

Much of this speculation was misplaced. Children did complain. Parents were concerned. But the implications were too monstrous to make sense and the parent's suspicions felt too paranoid to share. And when any parent voiced an alarm, anyone who heard felt an obligation to be reassuring, counter-alarming. Police reports of the initial investigation reconstruct a picture of the conventional behavior to be expected of children and parents when they are faced with a treacherous caretaker: normal parents will not allow themselves to perceive such a paralyzing betrayal.

Several misgivings were common to most of the parents. It was not unusual to knock for several minutes, sometimes five to ten minutes, before Iliana would come to the door. Sometimes she was in a robe, explaining she had been in the shower. Sometimes she had come from the bedroom, and on two reported occasions a naked child trailed after her. Sometimes Iliana warned that a child would probably be tired for want of a nap. And children often were tired, sleeping deeply through dinnertime, difficult to rouse. One mother might confess to a suspicion her child was being drugged, but another would remind her how hard kids play and how tired they can get. One night a couple was alarmed enough to call their doctor to request a blood test. By the time the doctor called back, the child was himself again, and the doctor said it was too late to find anything in the blood (apparently no one thought of a urine test). One three-year-old boy returned from his first day and went into a corner to bang his head on the wall.

Galloping diaper rash was common, as well as fecal staining for children already toilet trained. Doctors reassured: Night terrors, clinging, regressive behavior, fear of leaving home—all symptoms were readily attributed to family conflicts and the stresses of adapting to a new community.

Iliana sometimes wore sunglasses in the morning. Some wondered if she had been beaten. Others thought she seemed tired, thin distracted. But mostly she was sweet and caring. And always so accommodating.

Most families had little contact with one another except for chance meetings at the doorstep, so there was little base for collective concern or joint decisions. An exception occurred when a four-year-old boy asked his mother to suck his pee pee...like Iliana does. The mother discounted the story but decided to withdraw the child. Another mother heard the story and decided that she would also stop using the service. Both mothers agreed to share nothing of their concerns with other parents for fear of encouraging false rumors and causing trouble. The second mother broke her vow by confiding in the community recreation director, even while instructing her not to tell anyone. The recreation director broke her promise and made an anonymous report to child protective services in May 1984. The worker who investigated the report went directly to Iliana without contacting any parents or children. She "Unfounded" the report on the basis of Iliana's pleasant disposition and a bogus license framed on the wall.

Rumors continued to build over the next three months. When police were notified it was not by a parent but through a coincidental connection. A reporter friend of one of the mothers took the initiative to share the rumors with the state's attorney in charge of sex crimes, someone she happened to know through her work. Police investigators responded the following day.

While several children denied any problem, six-year-old "Jason" described what sounded like an unlikely combination of naked games and coercive sexual acts initiated by Frank Fuster. Jason's early insistence that he had seen, but not participated, changed in subsequent interviews to admissions of abject victimization by both Frank and Iliana as well as being forced to initiate sex with other younger children. Eventually some twenty-seven children described grotesque sexual exploitation.

"Jaime" the seven-year-old natural son of Frank Fuster, had a tender protective relationship with his stepmother and a staunch loyalty to his father. While he acknowledged seeing naked little kids chanting "ka-ka pee-pee" he denied that he or his parents were involved. Eventually he described wanton violence, bondage and torture inflicted by his father on Iliana and himself both in private and in contact with the other children.

One six-year-old girl provided an exception to the emerging pattern of horrors. In each of several sessions she was happy and apparently candid in her reassurances that she merely watched television during her visits. Since she was known to have visited the Fusters only twice and only for a few hours each time there was every reason to hope she had really been spared. But other children named her as a victim. In an agonizing display of shame, she finally demonstrated how she was stripped and humiliated by Frank in a circle of jeering, naked children.

Jason, the only child to make incriminating statements to the first police officers, described videotaping to the Bragas. Sometimes, he said children were shown the tapes from previous experiences as a warm-up for the rituals of the day. No equipment or tapes were found when the house was searched. Jaime said his uncle had carried away a car full of materials the night before. Several unusual photos were left behind, including one of a mask and others of both Manuel and Iliana profusely soiled with feces. Also confiscated was a wooden crucifix found under the mattress in the master bedroom.

During the trial in August and September of 1985, children testified in the judge's chambers. There were disturbing inconsistencies and contradictions, especially on cross-examination. Two defense experts Ralph Underwager, a Minnesota psychologist, and Lee Coleman, a child psychiatrist from California gave depositions discrediting the methods and the interpretations of the Bragas' videotaped interviews. Coleman's courtroom testimony was scathing. He denounced the testimony of the Bragas. He attacked the use of anatomic dolls. He stigmatized any reassurances offered to the children by the Bragas or by the parents. He linked their belief in the children to prejudice against the defendants. He challenged the credibility of any child led into sexual disclosures in repeated clinical play sessions. He said that legitimate victims would complain immediately of painful mistreatment and that it was extremely unlikely that descriptions of coprophagia and blood ritual could be factual. Defense played for the jury the entire body of interview tapes to expose the Bragas' supposedly manipulative techniques.

Even as the tapes ground on in the courtroom Iliana was recording a deposition prior to testifying against her husband. With no plea bargains or promises she had decided to plead guilty to all counts against her. Although pleading guilty to the acts charged, she said she did not molest the children. "I couldn't do something like that. Frank made me do those things." That split self-concept of innocence is the apparent basis for the paradoxical polygraph examinations. It also offers a clue to the apparently comfortable denials of some of the children. The slave-like mentality and behavior she describes is reminiscent of the dissociative creation of non-participant alternate identities typically seen in survivors of child sexual abuse.

Iliana's accounts in deposition and testimony give a rare adult-participant glimpse into a surreal world usually described only by children. She describes being tricked and raped into submissive terror by Frank at sixteen while she was visiting her mother from her native Honduras. Frank's threats to expose her shame to her family and his showdown with her parents in claiming her as a bride draw on the classic old-world philosophy of the virgin-whore dichotomy and the Sicilian tradition of rape and marriage.

The wedding in late September 1983, set off a relentless progression of forced sexual humiliation and tests of submission. Frank began offering her as a baby sitter within three months of the wedding, just after Iliana's seventeenth birthday.

Iliana gave graphic endorsement of the children's tales of drugs, urine, feces, masquerade, terror, animal slaughter and perverted rituals. It became obvious that Frank spent most of his days in sexual contact with the children. She also described nighttime orgies of drugs, bloody anal rape (the crucifix confiscated from under the mattress was used to induce bleeding) and bondage. She acknowledged savage beatings of Jaime, as well as herself, including at least one time when Jaime was suspended by the ankles and used as a human punching bag.

The children's stories about the pennies took on new credibility when Iliana described Frank's demands to be fussed over in the role of a baby with soiled diapers. The children were forced to prime him for these scenes with rectal suppositories which came wrapped in copper foil. Such bizarre regressive fetishes might be predicted in any man filled with so much primitive rage. In the punitive skepticism of a criminal inquiry and in the obstinate naiveté of the world or normal adults, however, such scenes are more comfortably attributed to the fantasies of children.

Another aspect worthy of study from Iliana's descriptions is the self-protective, dissociative behavior of children involved in such horrors. Even in the midst of violent interchanges between adults and sadistic molestation of individual children, other children continued to play with their toys as if nothing were happening. Children accepted sexual assaults passively, even continuing to play with a toy in the midst of assault. In game situations or when instructed to do so by Frank or Iliana, children would perform sex acts on one another, returning again to non-sexual play as if nothing had happened.

Frank Fuster was found guilty on all counts charged, with more than a lifetime of consecutive penalties. Iliana was sentenced to ten years. There is no systematic effort to study the ultimate effects on the children.

Note: Roland Summit has actively participated in one day seminars designed to help parents cope with the effects of the Little Rascals case.

In the "Miami Vice" case, also known as "Country Walk," Frank Fuster allegedly had a previous record of sexual assault on a juvenile ten years earlier and he left court after the guilty verdict proclaiming his innocence and the travesty of the judicial system.

The new United States Attorney General, Janet Reno, prosecuted the "Country Walk Case."

CONCLUSION: In the 1990s, cases easily verifiable as sexually exploitative of children, by anyone's standards, continue to abound. Polly Klaas was snatched from her bedroom and killed. Wesley Allen Dodd asked to be hung for his sexual assault and killing of young victims. A pedophile caught in Indiana for sexually assaulting a child at the child's home while her parents slept admitted to doing this across the country. And, a store clerk in Fairfax, Virginia, was caught red-handed sexually assaulting and videotaping children while their parents shopped.

The lesson to learn: Denial will assure the future of these activities and the truth must be known if children are to be effectively protected.

When a child told her parent early during the Little Rascals case that a defendant threatened to kill her cat, the parent did not consider it a small coincidence when dead kittens showed up on her doorstep. Children must be properly understood if they are going to receive appropriate protection.

QUESTIONS AND ANSWERS

These are the most frequently asked questions about child sexual abuse and the Little Rascals case. The answers relate to many of the ideas and materials already exposed in this book and will provide a proper summation to a terrible subject that we must begin to understand—Crimes Against Children.

Is child sexual abuse a problem in this country? If so, to what extent?

Yes. The issues surrounding all forms of child abuse and neglect have been denied and hidden from public view for generations. Only recently have people been willing to admit that children should be treated as people and not property. Yet, many still believe "children should be seen and not heard." It is estimated that ten to twenty-five percent of the child population is sexually molested by age eighteen. With these statistics and dehumanizing characterizations of children from past generations, those who would molest children have found their bounty.

What are the greatest challenges dealing with child sexual abuse?

Society's denial and individual denial are issues that prevent proper intervention and solution. There are cases where people admit to the alleged actions but refuse to realize they are abusive. In one case a perpetrator (related to the child as is usually the case) saw nothing wrong with French kissing the child. Another considered it appropriate to spank the child's penis for wetting its diaper.

Legislators struggle to provide sufficient resources. However, until laws are written to mandate maximum CPS caseloads at a level of twelve to eighteen cases, Social Services intervention will be reduced to a bureaucratic jungle of paperwork and file cabinets. Society must be willing to pay the price tag for child protection.

Is child abuse increasing or just being reported more often?

Society is finally willing to define child abuse in a way that covers many more issues than it did in the past. Naturally, with this coverage, more abuse is reported than before. However, there was plenty of abuse in the past and I am optimistic that the increase of reports is a sign of the times—seeking solutions to a problem that has always existed.

I do wish to note that a great deal of cases categorized as neglect or inappropriate discipline may be borderline abuse. In either case, many times the problems result from a lack of knowledge dealing with typical childhood issues. Yet it is not an excuse for a child becoming injured.

Consequently, it is strongly recommended that parents read and learn as much as they can. A minimum of twelve years of schooling is required just to enter the workplace. Raising children is one of the hardest jobs I've ever undertaken. It stands to reason, parents cannot do it alone and they should feel they can receive help from outside resources.

I can look at my own life and understand issues that were written off in the past as "just part of growing up." Now, I realize some of those events should not have been part of a child's life.

Is there a witch-hunt concerning alleged perpetrators of sex crimes? Can we believe the children? Do false accusations occur?

Perpetrators of sexual crimes have traditionally avoided detection and prosecution. The new approaches to successfully detect and prosecute have resulted in more publicity and the perception that the prisons must be crowded with innocent people accused of sexual abuse of children. There are innocent people in jail for all kinds of crimes—but no more for sexual crimes than any other crime.

You can believe the children, but you need to make sure you understand what they are saying before you jump to conclusions. A sexually abused child once stated, "Uncle Henry did it." She was referring to the hurting caused by a venereal disease. Uncle Henry was arrested, but further investigation found a neighbor who cunningly referred to his penis as Uncle Henry while abusing the child. Needless to say, the "real" Uncle Henry was cleared.

My experience with false accusations is personal. At age ten, I returned home from baseball practice with my Oriental coach one evening while living in Hawaii. An Oriental couple occupied the doorway of my home telling my parents that their four-year-old daughter complained of a white "haole" boy pulling down her underwear that afternoon.

My coach explained that I had been with him all afternoon. The couple left, realizing it must have been another "haole." Few "haoles" lived in that neighborhood. I was just glad I had not been anywhere near my home that afternoon. It was so frightening, I even remember what I had for dinner that evening—delicious spaghetti. While the child probably was not lying or fantasizing about someone committing the act, the parents were accusing wrongly on the presumption of racial association.

Do social workers overreact or underreact?

Like any profession, there are varying levels of skill and knowledge among social workers. However, the nature of this profession means the worst can occur even under the best circumstances, and someone always has the opinion that "it could have been handled differently."

Some believe social workers should place most children involved in CPS investigations out of their parents' custody. Others believe social workers should leave everyone alone, giving parents a license to raise children anyway they deem appropriate.

Social workers should be careful to avoid these two extreme camps. "Baby Snatchers" are just as dangerous as social workers who willingly believe the crafty explanations of potential perpetrators.

The "reasonable effort" law governing social work is based on the knowledge that making efforts to keep families intact will better serve the interests of children in the long term. The best social work attempts to avoid placing children in the foster care system, but moves swiftly and effectively during the investigative stage so that the truth can be known and children can be protected.

It is possible to receive a new investigation every other day over extended periods of time and still maintain a caseload level below twelve. Unfortunately, many social services agencies are not provided with the after-care treatment staff needed to maintain this appropriate caseload level.

What role does the media play? Is it fair?

The media can help educate the public. However, the media is comprised of the same public that is not well-educated about child sexual abuse. One major lesson has been learned about the media. It is extremely powerful and you really should learn everything you can about a subject beyond the media coverage if you wish to make a comprehensive assessment of the issues involved. The media attempts to be fair, but it is limited by its one-dimensional parameters in a three-dimensional world.

The media took a more responsible position in the Little Rascals case than it did in the McMartin case. At the Farmville trial, the media cooperated by sharing information with each other and approaching people with the respect and dignity that fits the polite Southern disposition of people in North Carolina. Most media representatives worked very hard to try and understand the issues on all sides of the case.

Certain editorial elements in the media, however, were not objective, responsible or dignified—merely misinformed. Fortunately, it only represented a small percentage of the media. Unfortunately it was the parents, their children and hard-working public servants who had to listen to the shallow insights.

How does one explain the fantastic stories and tales of young preschool children in allegations of sexual abuse that occur in large cases like the McMartin case in California or the Little Rascals case in North Carolina?

Experts ten years ago would say "believe the child." Today's expert should say "understand the child."

1. There is a basis to every child's statement, a central truth.

2. The basis may be a personal experience of the child, something the child has seen or heard or a meshing of several experiences with one another (like dreams, make believe play or a whole collection of past experiences or ideas that are a part of the child's history).

3. A child may give a wrong answer or a whole series of wrong answers, even naming people who may not be involved

because the child really does not understand the extent of the incidents. Tell the child it's okay to say, "I don't know."

Suggestive questioning can influence a child, but far more mistakes are made by interviewers who fail to understand the basis of the child's statement. Influencing the child to change the central facts is more difficult than one may realize, especially in a one-hour interview.

A good investigator should still be able to ascertain the central truth or, at least, realize the answer is somewhere in the scope of a complete law enforcement investigation. The investigator should use collateral information from medical evidence, polygraphs, corroborating witness statements and even information from the alleged perpetrator to reach the truth. I have obtained confessions from perpetrators who said something like, "Hey, I did some of that stuff, but not everything you say I did!"

4. Understanding the basis for the child's statements will ultimately clear a false accusation or substantiate the allegations against the perpetrator.

Statements by children in the Little Rascals case saying some of the alleged events occurred on "spaceships" does make sense. When investigators understood the children were taken away from the day care center in the fall of 1988 to go to the Chowan County Fair where the children participated in spaceship rides, they realized this provided the opportunity to take the children elsewhere for the commission of the alleged crimes.

5. Many perpetrators will do things to cover their tracks. Influencing children with fantasy stories or make believe incidents will create a more fantastic sounding disclosure. Sometimes, the perpetrator does this not even realizing the benefit to him or her. When the perpetrator lies to the child for the purpose of threat or coercion, these false stories may become a part of the child's disclosure.

How can child abuse end?

1. Prevention programs, like the early intervention program established in Hawaii for nearly twenty years, prepare new parents with the skills they need to properly care for their children. Many non-profit groups, like the National Committee to Prevent Child Abuse, advocate successful prevention programs like this.

2. Social Services programs need to utilize volunteer parent mentors in the community who can work with treatment cases if the government is not willing to pay for these necessary services.

Also, special task forces to deal with the most serious cases need to be established to remedy the bureaucracy. On a daily basis filling out forms and paperwork, risk assessments and diagrams for each case slows investigations and ties the hands of social workers, allowing too many children to slip between the cracks.

3. Parents and professionals working with children need to be educated—not only about children, but also about the dynamics of child abuse and neglect issues. This includes knowledge of the child protection system—the courts, law enforcement, social services, day care, medical services, mental health, education and family counseling services.

4. Chronic abusers, like pedophiles, need to remain separate from children. Some people advocate more rehabilitation programs for these sex offenders. Others advocate more prosecution and longer prison terms. Still others advocate that offenders be required to notify new neighbors after leaving prison. And, some people advocate for paroled offenders to be monitored with polygraph machines. The trends are clear—the public is beginning to understand that the chronic child abuser, like any addict, notoriously repeats his or her crime. Action is finally taking place.

5. Child abuse, neglect and dependency statutes need to be reviewed on a regular basis to assure that they are protecting this nation's smallest citizens—the children. The Mary Ellen case was the first child abuse case in America to go to court. This occurred in 1874. Advocates used a "cruelty to animals" law in New York to win that case because no child abuse law existed at that time. One hundred and twenty-one years is not a very long time for recognizing, understanding and defeating child abuse and neglect—but it is a beginning.

What other allegations causing suspicion evolved in the Little Rascals case?
Some other allegations were:

1. Robert Kelly made car payments for a defendant, Dawn Wilson.

2. Robert Kelly's plumbing van was often seen at a marina where a suspected boat docked. It later sank.

3. Dawn Wilson visited a mental health professional soon after the center closed and long before her arrest.

4. Scott Privott inquired with others about entering the child pornography business.

5. Scott Privott had been accused in at least one previous sex crime.

6. Betsy Kelly continued to operate and expand the center even though tax records showed it operating at a deficit.

7. Neighbors observed Scott Privott stripping out the interior of his van after the investigation began.

8. Neighbors viewed significant activity in the upstairs of the day care center the evening after investigators notified the owners of the investigation.

Did the Little Rascals case get out of control?

The Little Rascals case was out of control when Bob Kelly was allegedly in the process of committing his crimes. Control was gained by competent authorities who successfully placed him in prison. Let's place the blame where it properly belongs—with Robert Fulton Kelly, Jr.

FINAL ARGUMENTS

The following is a summation of the child sexual abuse issue. It is my own final argument that I would have presented at the trial of Robert Fulton "Mr. Bob" Kelly, Jr. if I had had the opportunity. I write it for all the Little Rascals children and all the children who must go to sleep at night with a deep, dark secret in their hearts.

Prior to January of 1989, tremendous storm clouds gathered around the Little Rascals Day Care Center in Edenton, North Carolina. Parents were having numerous behavioral problems with their children that the defense would like you to believe were just natural stages resulting from normal family issues.

In fact, most of these parents made every effort to rationalize many of these problems as stages. Most parents refused to believe that these severe behavior problems could be attributed to abuse by Kelly. For three months, some sent flowers to the Kellys, paid extra to keep the center open and tried to convince their children that allegations of abuse were false.

I shudder to think of the problems and suffering that would not have received treatment if the proper diagnosis had not been made in this case—the diagnosis that these weren't natural stages, but the result of abuse by Robert Fulton Kelly, Jr. Can you imagine treating heart disease with a diagnosis of heartburn?

What would be happening to the lives of these children if the disclosures never came? What serious effects of lost innocence would these children suffer as adults if they had not been referred to proper health care professionals? Where would all the children be if the allegations were kept secret? Where would the children be if a child had not said to its mother, "Mr. Bob plays with little boys' ding dongs and hineys," or if another child had not said to its mother, "Mr. Bob put his finger in my bottom," or if another child had not said to its mother, "Mr. Bob put his ding dong in my mouth."

I could continue, but I think the point is made. The symptoms were there. The disclosures were there; and yes, more disclosures came as children were referred to therapists they so desperately needed—therapists who gave a healthy, safe place for the children to speak.

The hardest thing in a case like this is putting a child on the stand. Adults have difficulty understanding what children are talking about; and children have difficulty talking to adults who don't understand. Discussions of witches, pirates and spaceships may be difficult to explain; but no explanation is needed for "Mr. Bob plays with little boys' ding dongs and hineys." The consistency in testimony by the children, their parents and investigators needs no explanation either. They are telling the truth.

Defense witnesses on the contrary seemed very inconsistent. Bob Kelly testified he never carried day care children in his plumbing van (other than his own child, niece and nephew). Later he told about the time the station wagon broke down and he transported many of the day care children in his plumbing van. One defense witness said Bob Kelly was rarely at the center. Another said she wondered why Kelly was at the center so often. Another defense witness one day stated the DSS report was completely inaccurate and on another day disclosed the information that was exactly in that report.

Many experts have testified in this trial and have given excellent advice on ideal investigations—the same ideals that the professionals involved in this case hold and practice.

One defense expert testified repeated interviews can hamper forensic data. Police officer Toppin joined the Social Services investigation to reduce the number of interviews. The Child Day Care Section investigation cooperated with this ideal as well by not reinterviewing the children. Leaking important facts to the investigation that could pollute the forensic data did not occur. A newspaper article on the case did not appear in the Edenton paper until three months after the Department of Social Services investigation ended.

Betsy Kelly testified she heard rumors, but it was later before she realized it was not a particular parent (name withheld) who made the allegations. Rumors naturally existed, but the facts of the case remained closely guarded, as they should be in a professional investigation. This investigation exemplifies the idealism the defense expert witnesses proclaimed.

There is one ideal here that is deficient; but it rests with many of the defense expert witnesses—an apparent lack of experience interviewing children. Although one medical expert testified he had examined several hundred sexual abuse victims and had previously testified only for prosecution cases, another defense expert testified he interviewed only three or four children under the age of six years. Another testified he interviewed ten victims of sexual abuse in ten years. Another testified she actually participated in only one study involving suggestibility of children.

Prosecution experts came from the University of North Carolina in Chapel Hill, which works with sexually abused children on a daily basis. A defense expert even relied on a UNC study.

You heard what Kelli De Sante (Bob Kelly's ex-wife) said about Bob Kelly—the child pornography, the dirty underwear, the sadistic treatment. Can one really believe Kelli De Sante made up these stories?

You heard what the children had to say about Bob Kelly—the molestation, the wild stories and the sadistic abuse.

Can one really believe the children were brainwashed to come to court two and a half years later to tell about the same incidents told to social workers in the earliest stages of the investigation?

The whole story concerning Robert Kelly's activities at Little Rascals may never be completely known, but these children have told you to the best of their ability about activities that in this state carry a life sentence. You cannot disregard their statements, just as social workers, parents and therapists could not disregard their disclosures. How many witnesses do you need to convict a person of a crime?

Some people still believe man has not walked on the moon because they believe it was all staged; and they have not been there themselves. Some people believe Kelly is innocent because they believe a conspiracy led to brainwashing of the children and because they did not see a video of the crimes being committed.

Man has walked on the moon and Robert Fulton Kelly, Jr. has committed "Crimes Against Children."

The Child Sex Crime Syndrome
By David McCall

1. The Denial—even when perpetrators confess, they often retract their confessions and usually minimize the traumatic nature of the incidence (s).

2. The Extreme Camps—Beliefs are unbalanced. People generally join one of three camps:

   Belief Camp #1. They say sex abuse is everywhere and always the cause of major behavior problems.

   Belief Camp #2. They say most allegations are false.

   Belief Camp #3. They say it happens, but not to anyone they trust and respect.

3. The Forgive and Forget Probability—The majority of spouses/caregivers ultimately support the perpetrator (who is usually someone close to the child) rather than the child victim.

4. The Domino Effect—Even when a case of sexual abuse is solved, the problems are just beginning. Everyone feels affected.

5. The Blame—Criticism and blame from family, friends and community are directed at the victim, the protective guardian and the system—rarely at the perpetrator.

6. The Healing—Starts when the child begins to feel he or she can trust others.

The Fortress

The soldiers snoring in their bunks,
The Captain makes his rounds.
He floats from door to door
Insuring regulation smoothness.
All is well, whisper the sleepy snores
And cracked doors. All is well.
The last silent door is locked.
Puzzled, he grips the knob with all his force.
Within, the frightened soldier cringes
At the insistent sound, rattling his dreams.
The captain wants in, but all is well!
The captain wants in.
The soldier breathlessly hopes the lock is strong,
But the metal grinds faster.
The soldier lies, his stiff body sandwiching the mattress
With the floor, praying for silence.
The fort heats up with the captain's rage
And the door burns down.
Melting from the captain's heat,
The soldier endures the abuse, patiently.

After the captain's erection of anger
Had fallen, he leaves the dazed soldier
And cracks the door as he exits
To finish his rounds.
All is well.

Written by T.J., incest survivor, at age 21. Her alleged perpetrator never saw jail during twelve years of sexual abuse, just the respect most retired U.S. military officers receive.

The old Little Rascals day care center operated from July, 1986 to August, 1988 under it's new owners Bob and Betsy Kelly.

The new Little Rascals day care center—a closed Double-cola bottling plant was renovated and opened in September, 1988 by Bob and Betsy Kelly.

The "Walking House" where some children stated they were taken by "Mr. Bob." This home belonged to Bob and Betsy Kelly—seven miles from the centers.

Drawing by a Little Rascals sex crime victim.

PUBLIC RECORD

The following items represent primary and secondary materials related to the Little Rascals case which are part of the public record.

REVOCATION OF CHILD DAY CARE LICENSE from the North Carolina Department of Human Resources to Mr. and Mrs. Robert Kelly, Little Rascals Owners, March 22, 1989. Public Record.

Dear Mr. and Mrs. Kelly:

Pursuant to General Statute 110-100 and General Statute 110-105.2, the Child Day Care Section, Division of Facility Services in the Department of Human Resources, hereby revokes the Child Day Care License, ID# 21-5-5024, issued to you to operate a day care facility.

On February 9, 1989, a representative of the Child Day Care Section visited your facility to investigate allegations of child sexual abuse and violations of the child day care licensing rule regarding discipline. During the visit, our representative discussed the allegations with appropriate staff and Ms. Betsy Kelly. Ms. Kelly denied all allegations. Since that visit, the investigation has continued and additional information gathered.

On February 9, 1989, the Chowan County Department of Social Services provided written notification to this agency that child sexual abuse was substantiated against a licensee during their investigation of the report. This agency concurs with that conclusion. In addition, the Child Day Care Section substantiated child neglect against a licensee. The investigation resulted in disclosure of the following information:

1. Several children have stated and demonstrated that they were sexually abused more than one time by a licensee.
2. Other children, who themselves were not abused, have stated they observed adults in the facility mishandling, mistreating or abusing children.
3. A parent has stated that he/she observed two different children being shaken by a licensee as a form of discipline.
4. A child has stated that the group of children to which she was assigned was often left unsupervised at naptime.
5. A licensee took children in a pickup truck on unauthorized outings. The vehicle did not meet transportation requirements.

Therefore, this agency concludes that your child day care license must be revoked. In addition, future issuance of a child day care license or registration to you is unlikely because of the child neglect substantiation.

You are further informed that if you wish to appeal this action, you have the right to request a contested case hearing in accordance with General Statute 150B, Article 3 and General Statute 110-90(5). You may request a contested case hearing by filing a verified petition at the Office of Administrative Hearings, Post Office Drawer 11666, Raleigh, North Carolina 27604, in accordance with General Statute 150B-23(a). The request must be received by the Office of Administrative Hearings within sixty days of receipt of this letter. If you do not request a contested case hearing within this time, you will lose your right to appeal this action.

If you request a contested case hearing according to the procedures described in the preceding paragraph, please send a copy of your letter (not the original) to Ms. (name omitted), 325 Salisbury Street, Raleigh, North Carolina 27611.

If you appeal this action, you must post this letter of revocation in a prominent place in your day care facility and the letter must remain posted until final action is determined as required by 10 NCAC 3U .2011(d) which states:

"If revocation is stayed pending appeal, the revocation order shall be posted in a prominent place in the center or home pending final action."

This agency remains available to assist you upon request. If you have questions or concerns about this matter, you may call the Raleigh office at (ph. #).

Sincerely,
Chief
Child Day Care Section/Division of Facility Services

SUBPOENAS to investigators, therapists and parents issued by the defense in the Robert Kelly Trial were challenged in court as being overburdensome. Here is a list of the requests made from those public documents. Those subpoenaed were initially requested to be in court for each day of the trial. Ellipses (...) represent words omitted for readability and to accommodate length.

Investigators and Therapists

To produce for the court, at the place, date and time indicated above, the following:

1. All records related to your interviews, evaluation, or examination of any of the named children...

2. All records as set forth in No. 1 above with respect to any child who attended the Little Rascals Day Care Center...

3. Copies of all publications, articles, or written materials authored by you.

4. Copies of your transcripts from each college or university attended by you...

5. Copies of any and all outlines...for speeches or oral presentations given by you since 1988.

6. Copies of any and all written office policies, manuals...

7. With regard to your evaluation, interview, or observation of any child who attended Little Rascals...all communications between you or your office and (goes on to name professionals involved in the case)...(i) any physician, psychiatrist, social worker, nurse, interviewer, counselor, or therapist not specifically named above.

8. Any and all photographs, pictures, newspaper articles or depictions of or concerning...

9. Copies of any and all receipts...of your attendance at continuing education or professional seminars for the period between 1985 and the present date.

10. Certificates or diplomas...

11. Appointment ledgers or calendars...

12. Any and all notes...or other items showing the name of each person who made referrals to you of the children who attended Little Rascals Day Care Center....

13. Copies of any reading materials...delivered by you or your agency to any of the parents of children...and which materials were related to the reports and investigations...

14. Any anatomical dolls, puppets, or props of any kind used by you or your agency...

Parents

1. Videotapes, audiotapes, transcripts, notes, diaries, or recordings of interviews, conversations (lists professionals) or other person involved in the investigation.

2. Copies of documents, letters, booklets received by you since June 1, 1988.

3. Notes, diaries, memoranda, reports...related to the Little Rascals.

4. Photographs, home movies.

5. Photographs, newspaper photos used by you and were used or shown to your child for identification.

6. Tapes, videos, books...related to the issue of child sexual abuse.

7. Dolls, props, puppets...used by you...in the discussions with your child about the accusations of child abuse in the Little Rascals day care cases.

8. Writings made by your child.

9. Records, receipts or other evidence of payments for any type of treatment.

10. Copies of lawsuits.

11. Copies of reports made by you to any law enforcement agent concerning allegations involving children who attended the Little Rascals Day Care Center.

12. Copies of reports from a doctor, psychologist, social worker...therapist.

13. Copies of affidavits...

14. Copies of...receipts...to Little Rascals Day Care Center, its owners or operators.

15. Complete medical records and psychological or therapeutic records for your child since the child's date of birth.

Issued this 5th day of July, 1991.

The subpoenas were indeed considered to be burdensome by the prosecution and motions to quash the subpoenas were repeatedly granted by Judge Marsh McLelland. His decision was upheld when it was appealed to higher courts by the defense attorneys. Financial sanctions (allegedly a first for a criminal case in North Carolina) made by Judge McLelland against the defense attorneys were not upheld.

EXCERPTS: MOTION TO QUASH SUBPOENA submitted by David McCall.

NOW COMES David McCall, Social Worker III, of the Chowan County Department of Social Services, by and through the undersigned attorney, moving the Court for an Order quashing a subpoena heretofore issued in these proceedings and respectfully shows unto the Court:

1. That your movant has been served...produce voluminous records...concerning a number of children listed therein that he has not seen or interviewed.
2. That your movant is directed...day to day for the entire term of the trial...
3. That it is...more than seventy-five miles...and it would be a financial...hardship...
4. That the defense would not present evidence until the state has rested...
5. That...the documents requested are highly confidential...
6. That the parents...have not given their consent...
7. That the testimony sought...is not relevant...
8. That the testimony...being the work product...is not producible over objection under the Work Product Privilege Doctrine.
9. That the testimony and documents...are not subject to disclosure under the provisions of Section 15A-904 of the General Statutes of North Carolina.
10. That the subpoena is broad, oppressive, unreasonable and shows on its face that the defendant seeks to engage in a "fishing expedition" which is not permitted by means of a subpoena duces tecum.

WHEREFORE, your movant respectfully prays that the Court quash the subpoena...

Your movant further prays that the Court enter an Order directing the defendant, Robert Fulton Kelly, Jr. to pay reasonable expenses and attorney fees resulting from the issuance of these subpoenas.

Appendix

Child Protective Services Report

INTAKE INFORMATION when receiving reports of Abuse, Neglect and Dependency. Abuse reports require the initiation of an investigation within 24 hours. Neglect reports require this within seventy-two hours. Dependency is a child with no parent or caregiver and should consequently require immediate attention.

Date, time, and type of report.

Name(s), age(s) and location of victim(s).

Name(s), address (work and home) and phone numbers of parents.

Perpetrator(s).

Direction(s).

Allegation—who, what, when, and where.

Previous history.

Family awareness of report?

Other people or agencies with information.

Reporter's goals.

Name/address/phone number of reporter(s). (Anonymous reports are taken. However, it is a serious infraction to knowingly make a false report.)

May be screened out or referred to another agency or:

Assigned to: Child Protective Services Investigator.

Outcome: Either substantiated or unsubstantiated after a complete investigation—which must include interviews with alleged victim(s) and alleged perpetrator(s), a home visit, and any other collateral information as necessary (such as medical exams, or other interviews with family, friends, teachers, etc.). Collaterals could be endless, so one must use appropriate judgement concerning when to stop. Rule of thumb would be the point and time when sufficient evidence exists to make a substantiation or unsubstantiation by the department.

In North Carolina, one must document all findings on a DSS form 1360 known as the "green sheet"(probably because the lined document is green) and complete basic data forms concerning client's name, age, race, sex, etc. Also, a form DSS 5104 is sent to the Department of Human Resources Central Registry with identifying information concerning the results of the investigation. In North Carolina the central registry tracks victims who may move throughout the state, but it did not track perpetrators until changes were made in 1994.

PUBLIC REACTION from "Frontline" Documentary that aired in May 1991.

There was a lot of negative reaction to a televised PBS program that aired in 1991. Similar reaction also occurred in

1992 when a follow-up program aired after Robert Kelly's conviction.

Parents produced a statement that criticized the program for allegedly giving the impression that the accusers were all well-to-do, when they were actually from a large cross-section; that three state therapists interviewed all the children when actually as many as eight "private" and "independent" counselors were involved; and that the show did not adequately clarify the limitations of the parents due to the pending trial.

"Frontline" followed up with a statement saying it felt the program was not biased and it portrayed a balanced view. One of its officials later allegedly went on record to say she felt the defendants were innocent, however; and the following excerpts from actual letters typify the majority of letters received in Edenton after the program aired.

"I believe nothing happened at the center. Mass hysteria has ruined the lives of the accused."

"Ms. (name omitted) should have her tongue cut off and be sued for accusing these innocent people."

"Edenton is a beautiful, historic town, but I wouldn't live there in a million years."

"After watching the documentary, I changed my mind 180 degrees. How could anyone believe these people are guilty."

"This case sounds just like the Salem Witch trials. I can't believe this has happened in the 20th Century."

The following is an excerpt from a letter written after Kathryn Dawn Wilson's conviction promoting a different point of view. This is reprinted with permission from the author, Betty Wade-Coyle, Executive Director, The Hampton Roads Chapter of the National Committee To Prevent Child Abuse.

In the Edenton, North Carolina, Little Rascals Day Care Center case, the prosecution has been careful and low-key. In fact, families of victims and others close to the trial have chosen not to try the cases in the press and, unfortunately, much of the material which has been published...reflects only one side of the cases.

...in a recent editorial, there has been some intimation that the jury system that has served our country well for over two centuries is somehow flawed. But the plain fact is that jurors who did not read newspaper accounts but heard the evidence in court convicted Robert Kelly of ninety-nine counts of abuse and, when individually polled at the time the verdict was returned, swore under oath that they found the defendant guilty as charged.

In Edenton, ninety children have now disclosed that they were abused at the Little Rascals Day Care Center. These children made their disclosures at different times, over a four-year period, to different counselors who were specially trained to interview and evaluate the validity of what the children were saying without influencing their answers.

...it is difficult for us to accept the fact that such abuse can happen, and our society finds it hard to admit that such terrible things can and do occur to our precious children, especially when some perpetrators appear to be trusted, upstanding citizens.

Currently, research on sexual abuse substantiates that one in four females and one in six males in our society will be sexually abused before their eighteenth birthdays. Sexual abuse of children in our society is an epidemic, and until each of us is willing to believe the children, to come to their aid and to publicly condemn, punish and treat the perpetrators, our communities and country will continue to pay the price of the myriad of social ills, crime and violence borne of sexual abuse.

Until each of us admits the gravity of the problem and begins to take action to stop child abuse in day care centers, in our schools and, yes, in our homes, none of our children will be safe.

Appendix
READING LIST

G. G. Abel, E. B. Blanchard, and J. Becker, "How a Molester Perceives the World," INTERNATIONAL JOURNAL OF LAW AND PSYCHIATRY, 7: 89-103, 1984.

Jan Boys, "Conditions Mistaken for Child Abuse," CHILD ABUSE, (Vol. and Date unknown), pp. 358-383.

P. Carnes, OUT OF THE SHADOWS: UNDERSTANDING SEXUAL ADDICTION, CompCare Publications, MN: 1983.

Robin Clark and Judith Clark, THE ENCYCLOPEDIA OF CHILD ABUSE, NY: Facts on File, Inc., 1989.

John Crewdson, BY SILENCE BETRAYED: SEXUAL ABUSE OF CHILDREN IN AMERICA, NY: Harper and Row Publishers, Inc., 1988.

Kimberly A. Crnich, J.D., and Joe Crnich, J.D., SHIFTING THE BURDEN OF TRUTH: SUING CHILD SEXUAL ABUSERS-A LEGAL GUIDE FOR SURVIVORS AND THEIR SUPPORTERS, Lake Oswego, OR: Recollex Publishing, 1992.

Billie Wright Dziech and Judge Charles B. Schudson, ON TRIAL: AMERICA'S COURTS AND THEIR TREATMENT OF SEXUALLY ABUSED CHILDREN. Boston: Beacon Press, 1989.

Mark D. Everson and Barbara W. Boat, "Putting The Anatomical Doll Controversy In Perspective: An Examination of The Major Uses and Criticisms of The Dolls In Child Sexual Abuse Evaluations." CHILD ıD NEGLECT, Vol. 8, No. 2, pp. 113-129,

ᴋelhor, Linda Williams, with Nanci Burns,
ᴌSERY CRIMES, Beverly Hills, CA: Sage
ᴌolications, Inc., 1988.

ᴀ L. Goldstein, THE SEXUAL EXPLOITATION OF
CHILDREN: A PRACTICAL GUIDE TO
ASSESSMENT, INVESTIGATION, AND
INTERVENTION, Elsevier, NY: Elsevier Science
Publishing Company, Inc., 1987.

Elizabeth Hollenberg, and Cynthia Ragan, CHILD SEXUAL
ABUSE: SELECTED PROJECTS, Prepared for the
National Center on Child Abuse and Neglect, Available
through the Clearinghouse on Child Abuse and Neglect,
1-800-394-3366, November, 1991.

Jan Hollingsworth, UNSPEAKABLE ACTS, NY: Congdon
and Weed, 1986.

D. Jones, "Reliable and Fictitious Accounts of Child Sexual
Abuse," JOURNAL OF INTERPERSONAL
VIOLENCE, Vol. No. 1987.

Terry Kellogg with Marvel Harrison, Foreword by B. J.
Thomas, BROKEN TOYS BROKEN DREAMS,
UNDERSTANDING AND
HEALING/CODEPENDENCY, COMPULSIVE
BEHAVIORS AND FAMILY, Amherst, MA: Brat
Publishing, 1990.

Duncan Lindsey, THE WELFARE OF CHILDREN, NY,
Oxford: Oxford University Press, 1994.

M. MacCulloch, P. R. Snowden, P. W. Wood, and H. E.
Mills, "Sadistic Fantasy, Sadistic Behavior and

Offending," BRITISH JOURNAL OF PSYCHIATRY, 143:20-29, 1983.

Dr. Ken Magid, THE HOLDING THERAPY HANDBOOK, Denver, Colorado.

Lisa Manshel, NAP TIME, NY: William Morrow and Company, Inc., 1990.

R. Mathews, J. Mathews, and K. Speltz, "Female Sexual Offenders: An Exploratory Study," Report from a study by the St. Paul Foundation, MN: 1988.

Lynn Jett Minick, THE VICTIM GOES TO COURT, Fayetteville, NC: People Assisting Victims, 1990.

James A. Monteleone and Armond E. Brodeur, CHILD MALTREATMENT: A CLINICAL GUIDE AND REFERENCE AND A COMPREHENSIVE PHOTOGRAPHIC REFERENCE IDENTIFYING POTENTIAL CHILD ABUSE, St. Louis, MO: G. W. Graphics and Publishing, 1994.

D. K. Runyan, et al., "Impact of Legal Intervention on Sexually Abused Children," THE JOURNAL OF PEDIATRICS, Vol. 113: pages 647-653, October, 1988.

Stanton Samenow, Ph.D., INSIDE THE CRIMINAL MIND, Toronto: Random House of Canada Limited, 1984.

Suzanne Somers, WEDNESDAY'S CHILDREN, NY: Putnam-Healing Vision Publishing, 1992.

B. Steele, "Lasting Effects of Childhood Sexual Abuse," CHILD ABUSE AND NEGLECT: THE INTERNATIONAL JOURNAL, Vol. No. 1985.

Gloria Steinem, REVOLUTION FROM WITHIN, NY: Little Brown, 1992.

Roland Summit, "The Child Sexual Abuse Accommodation
    Syndrome," CHILD ABUSE AND NEGLECT,
    7:177-193.

Debra Whitcomb, WHEN THE VICTIM IS A CHILD,
    Washington D.C.: National Institute of Justice, 1992.

Jerry L. Wyckoff, Ph.D. and Barbara C. Unell,
    DISCIPLINE WITHOUT SHOUTING OR SPANKING:
    PRACTICAL SOLUTIONS TO THE MOST COMMON
    PRESCHOOL BEHAVIOR PROBLEMS, Deephaven,
    MN: Meadowbrook Press, 1984.

Jerry L. Wyckoff, Ph.D. and Barbara C. Unell, HOW TO
    DISCIPLINE YOUR SIX TO TWELVE YEAR OLD:
    WITHOUT LOSING YOUR MIND, NY: Doubleday,
    1991.

RESOURCE AND REFERRAL SERVICES

Child Help USA...(800)-4-A-CHILD

Family Violence Prevention Fund.................(800) 777-1960

National Resource Center on Child
Sexual Abuse .... (800) 543-7006

National Center for the Prosecution
of Child Sexual Abuse.................................(703) 739-0321

National Center for Missing and
Exploited Children......................................(703) 235-3900

National Committee to Prevent
Child Abuse ....(312) 663-6520

National Victims Resource Center ....(800) 627-6872

Prevent Child Abuse, NC.............................(800) 354-KIDS

North Carolina Child Advocacy Institute......(919) 834-6623

American Professional Society
on the Abuse of Children............................. (312) 544-0166

The Children's Defense Fund.......................(202) 707-3000

Your Local Area 911

    In honor of the written contributors to this project (a project that would have been very difficult to complete without their generous help) a portion of the proceeds from sales of this book are being donated in the interests of children.

About the Author...

David E. McCall is a social worker currently serving as a child protective services investigator in North Carolina. Since his college years, when he worked with families on a Navajo reservation, he has partipated in various educational and advocacy programs for children. McCall was an investigator in the infamous Little Rascals day care case, which garnered him national attention and inspired him to write about child sexual crimes. Since then he has worked on several other multiple-victim/multiple-perpetrator child sexual abuse cases and hundreds of other physical abuse, sexual abuse and neglect cases.

Thirty-seven-year-old McCall has written about his social work experience in *Crimes Against Children* to empower readers with knowledge about sexual abuse crimes inflicted upon our innocent children. McCall lives in Northeastern, North Carolina, with his wife and son.